C000148598

AVP
ALIEN VS. PREDATOR™
THE CREATURE EFFECTS OF ADI

ALEC GILLIS and TOM WOODRUFF, JR.

designstudio|PRESS

DEDICATION

This book is dedicated to the many talented special effects artists who inspired us when we were kids, our parents who helped us along the way when we were young, and our own children who stayed behind while we went off to Prague to play with our monsters. Thank you Camille, Devon, Grace, Bella, David, Taylor, and Connor.

And to our wives, Alaine and Tami, who were with us and supported us along the way and through all the years as we each matured from prom dates to grown men who play with puppets, this book is lovingly dedicated.

Book design, captions, and digital tongue removal by Chris Ayers.

Photography by Jurgen Volmer, Tom Woodruff, Jr., Chris Ayers, and that Czech guy who wasn't supposed to be taking pictures anyway.

Published by Design Studio Press
8577 Higuera Street
Culver City, CA 90232
www.designstudiopress.com
E-mail: Info@designstudiopress.com

Printed in Hong Kong
First Edition, August 2004

Softcover ISBN 0-9726676-5-2
Library of Congress Control Number: 2004107546

Hardcover ISBN 0-9726676-6-0

Just as a motion picture cannot be made without the hundreds of people both onscreen and behind the scenes, this book is the result of the tireless and talented efforts of one of the largest crews we've ever had the pleasure to work with, the names of whom appear later in this volume. It is their work, which is always art turned into commodity, as it must be for movies. It is their work, which must be summoned up in sixty and seventy-hour workweeks, sometimes overnight, sometimes through the weekends. It is their drawings and sculptures and paintings. It is their molds and mechanisms and rubber skins and lycra-reinforced suit closures. It is their *art*, which is presented on the pages that follow.

We also must point out that we would not be such a big part of these films if not for our friend and mentor, Stan Winston, who showed us the way and foolishly turned over the keys. If we didn't say it then, we say it now, "Thank you, Stan, with love."

In addition, the decision of Twentieth Century Fox to produce this film must be acknowledged with thanks to, among others, Tom Rothman, Jon Davis, and Mike Hendrickson. Without the film, there would be no book and you would be looking at your empty hands right now.

We had the support of Tom Hammel and Chris Symes during the four-month shoot in Prague and we will still "exchange Christmas cards" with Adam Goodman, figuratively, if not through the mail.

Thanks also to Scott Robertson of Design Studio Press, and Debbie Olshan and Twentieth Century Fox Publicity for making this book possible.

And finally, in the last position before the picture starts, we thank Paul W. S. Anderson for having us on his picture and for his enthusiastic gasps from behind the monitors as our creatures performed for the cameras. His love and excitement for the *Alien* and *Predator* genres was infectious and reminded us that, for all the long hours and hard work, we really are lucky to be a part of all this. We were glad to deliver the "general unpleasantness" he requested....

If you stop long enough in this life to look around, you realize we are trapped in the same generation. The people you know and have come to respect are IT. The only it.

Like old tintypes, we all will eventually fade into oblivion, but not the works we leave behind.

Tom, Alec, and I have spent years on smoke-filled sets, being chased or pursuing something from one town or planet to another, wrapped in creations that would scare the life out of Satan himself.

The writer utters the mythology, the actor legitimizes it, and Tom and Alec make the director's choices physically tangible. Capable.

They are the Masters of the Impossible.

AVP is the latest...Herculean. Stretched to the limitless.

It has been an honor to enter their domain.

                                        – Lance Henriksen

HISTORY

And So It Begins...Again.

1979. The original *Alien*. At twenty years old, we had each already decided that we were going to make monsters for the movies. Of course, we hadn't done it by then–we didn't even know each other. Alec was on the West Coast, and Tom was on the East. We had each followed a similar path: liking the same movies (*Planet of the Apes*), each wanting to be the next Ray Harryhausen, and both of us making our own Super-8 movies.

But we were both there at opposite ends of the country, sitting in theatres and watching the same movie–the movie that would more than make its mark as a pinnacle of science-fiction films. As it turned out, *Alien* also served to inspire many talented, professional effects artists working today, as well as earn a position of honor amidst a legion of fans.

Alec was already in Los Angeles with a foot in the door. Tom was three years and three thousand miles away (it wouldn't be until 1982 that he would make the trip across country). Alec had the good fortune to be watching with Jim Cameron in Los Angeles, while Tom watched with his friend, Hutch, in Williamsport, Pennsylvania (Who? – Don't tell us you've never heard of Jim Cameron!).

We were both captivated by the style of Ridley Scott and the suspense and tension he created in that ominous, claustrophobic set. We were thrilled by H.R. Giger's Alien and Ridley Scott's making the most of what he showed of that creature and, more importantly, what he chose to hide. Of course

neither of us could have known that we would end up intertwined with the Alien legacy.

By 1985, when Twentieth Century Fox decided to move forward with the next installment, *Aliens*, we were both working at the studio of Stan Winston, where we met. We worked together on a number of films there and found our common interests and shared tastes in monsters, effects, and filmmaking. We moved to London for eight months, along with Stan and other key members of his staff; Shane Mahan, John Rosengrant, Richard Landon, and Rick Lazzarini.

Stan Winston has always had an enormous capacity to evaluate a person's strengths and assemble a very strong talent pool. He was also secure enough to trust his instincts. Stan had built his team over a period of two years, and by the time we started *Aliens*, he was confident enough to be able to place a great deal of responsibility upon us to work on the show as his Alien effects coordinators.

It was all such an amazing time! Although the work we do today is still very "hands-on", back then our hands were on *everything*. It was not only unusual, but in many cases expected that you would sculpt, make molds, run rubber, finish and paint, and perform with puppets and effects pieces on set.

One of Tom's first jobs was to sculpt the Alien head and egg. Fox sent a crate to Winston's studio and inside was one of the Giger heads from *Alien*, beautifully airbrushed and finished, which became

Opposite: After having battled each other on the pages of comic books, Aliens and Predators come face-to-face for the first time on the big screen in *AVP*.

Above: A sarcophagus containing a Predator arsenal is discovered in an ancient pyramid buried deep beneath the polar ice of Antarctica.

Left: After a fourteen-year absence, a Predator ascends to the silver screen once more.

Opposite: On set in Prague, the *AVP* crew prepares to film a close encounter of the Alien kind.

reference, as well as Jim Cameron's direction that the translucent rounded dome be removed for his film. Alec's first job was to sculpt the facehugger, referring to photos and frame blow-ups from the first film along with photos from Giger's own book of his work on *Alien*.

One of the early effects upon which we collaborated was the body of Bishop, torn in half by the Alien Queen. While John Richardson worked out a spring-loaded detaching plate for the waist, we lifecast Lance Henriksen, playing Bishop, and created the replica that would be split and tossed aside as the stowaway Queen exits the dropship. The same upper half would be used for scenes of Bishop's upper torso hitting and sliding across the floor of the ship, the *Sulaco.*

When we finished all the necessary pieces, we took them to the stage for Cameron's approval. We climbed up onto the four-foot rostrum from which he was shooting to proudly show off our handiwork. "Throw it on the floor." We couldn't have heard him right, we were proud of all the detail…the glass eyes! "I'm serious, throw it on the floor. That's the way it's going to be shot." We gingerly laid it on the floor, face-up, still looking for that gleam of approval in Cameron's eye. If there had been a soft, padded sound blanket nearby, we probably would have used that to cushion it from the harsh studio floor. "Gimme it." We handed it back to Cameron and watched the wind-up. He executed a perfect "piledriver" and the Bishop torso hit the floor face first and skidded a few feet away. "Yeah, that'll work."

Luckily it ended up face down so the initial damage was undetectable. Luckily Cameron had things to shoot and we had a Lance Henriksen face to repair. To this day it resides in the esteemed collection of Bob Burns, its eyes still bugging out of its head as if it remembers the ordeal.

Despite the difficult physical working conditions as we huddled in front of propane heaters, working off of shipping crates turned upside down to become tables, it is all remembered with great affection–like childbirth.

In 1990, Gordon Carroll, one of the producers of the first two pictures, called to ask if we were interested in creating the effects for *Alien*^{3}. The plan was to return to Pinewood Studios outside of London and he wanted someone who knew the drill. By now, we had formed our own company, Amalgamated Dynamics, Inc.

Also by this time, Tom had a small list of credits for playing monsters we designed and we went to the producers with the notion that it made the most sense for him to play the Alien. Tom had experience inside suits and we had a complete set of body molds that would allow us to start work immediately. The producers as well as the director, David Fincher, supported our notion.

Alien^3 allowed us to start from scratch on the Alien, and we turned to Giger's original art in his own books, wanting to stay true to his vision and to what the audience responded in the earlier films. To that end, we created a much more detailed, form-fitting body suit finished in the warm sepia tones of some of Giger's illustrations.

We also created eggs, facehuggers, and chest-bursters, all staples of the Alien lifecycle now firmly entrenched in the audience's expectations. And we had the opportunity to create the Animatronic head of Bishop, working once again with Lance Henriksen who provided a lifecast and voiced the dialogue to which our Animatronic was programmed to play back. The puppet head was remarkable in that it featured a translucent urethane skin, which was very new for its time, expertly finished by Yuri Everson and painted by Gino Acevedo and superbly mechanized by our mechanical designer for that effect, Dave Nelson.

Fincher and Sigourney Weaver put a definitive ending to the franchise as Ripley sacrifices herself to the fiery furnace of the leadworks, taking the Queen Alien embryo with her.

And then, in 1996, the story was developed in which enough DNA source material was recovered to

make it possible to clone Ripley. Disastrous for the future, but lucky for us, that material was tainted with enough Alien DNA coding to create the bridge that allowed us to bring back the Alien in all its many forms.

This time around, we'd stay home to both build and shoot the extensive list of Alien elements to be created. This afforded us the ability to rely on the talent pool we had become familiar with here in Los Angeles, as well as the resources of suppliers and vendors who provided access to everything we use from skin materials to Animatronic components. The efficiency of the build was enhanced by not having to put together and crew a temporary shop facility in another country nor crate and ship Animatronic characters and effects rigs overseas for shooting. But we were right in the middle of a move to a larger facility, having outgrown the shop space in which we started many years earlier. In fact, the sculpture of the new Alien was started in the old shop, then transported by truck to our new shop where it was completed.

We had wanted to make some revisions to the Alien for the new movie, both in appearance and approach. As it was genetically linked to its predecessor, we had to remain loyal to certain features. The general overall proportions and the specific extended foot which is a carry-over from the dog-leg-like configuration of the previous incarnation. But we made it more wicked in appearance, narrowing the front of the domed head and face and bringing the design lines to more of a point that lead right to the teeth and mouth. We also lifted the sternum and brought it out from the torso more to exaggerate the ribcage and comparatively de-emphasize the stomach. We made the hands longer, giving the extended palm more mass to help lengthen the arms. The four peg-like extensions were added to the back, this time articulated for a strange organic undulation, which ended up playing in only one scene. Because our director, Jean-Pierre Jeunet, was having some major sequences play underwater, a fin-like extrusion

was added to the tail to mimic the silhouette of a swimming crocodile's tail, also requiring us to water-proof the Animatronic Alien heads.

You can't make an Alien movie without breaking a few eggs, and improvements were also designed into the Alien eggs. For a key scene in which the Alien egg is revealed, we added a whole new organic articulation to the egg itself, making it pulsate and undulate with its entire body that was internally sectioned to provide multiple points of stretch and movement. Meanwhile, the four petals that open at the top would curl away elegantly, also making use of lips, which were articulated with bladders to close tightly. Even the interior of the egg was lined with more bladders to provide an organic life within.

Facehuggers, chestbursters, synthetics (the new "Call" line), and the like were similarly tuned-up in an effort to continue to hone the creatures with every opportunity. In addition, the Queen Alien had her second appearance in the series, made practical by the fact that Bob Burns had the original head from *Aliens* all those years ago. Bob was a creature-builder and suit performer himself, but much more—he is also a fan of every slimy or hairy or tentacled thing that was ever to creep, or crawl, or stalk across a movie screen. Today he is still the world's biggest monster fan and legitimate source of knowledge and has turned most of his home into a vast display of artifacts from over seventy years of monster movies, which he painstakingly maintains with the diligence of a museum curator.

Time was not on our side to even attempt to further develop the Queen Alien, but Bob allowed us to use the original head with a newly revised paint scheme. The original ten-year-old molds from London for the arms, legs, and tail were located at a replica company in Colorado, but the body and head molds were destroyed beyond use. The body was going to be huge and distended from bearing its offspring in a twisted human variation of the Alien life-cycle, so duplication of the original was not an issue.

The failed experimental clones that were

Top to Bottom: The creature from the original *Alien*; a rehearsal shot from *Aliens*, the transparent head dome returns in *Alien³*; a scene from the fourth installment of the franchise, *Alien Resurrection*.

Opposite: The Aliens of *AVP* are similar to their last incarnation as seen in *Alien Resurrection*, however some sculptural and color modifications were made.

Ripley's predecessors in the film were among the most fun from a creative design point of view, as was the new story element of the creature born of the Queen Alien, simply dubbed the Newborn.

The Newborn's entire configuration made it impossible as a man-in-a-suit for any aspects on set. Instead, the eight-foot tall creature was built completely as an Animatronic character, powered by a combined system of electronics and hydraulics and making use of a custom computer-driven motion control system. A quarter-scale articulated miniature was also designed and built for wide shots of the creature moving around the hold of the ship, but ultimately was never shot for the film.

Was there more to be done after *Alien Resurrection*? Absolutely. As is always the case, we have our own ideas and plans of where we would go with the next step of any creature or monster we create. Whether it ever gets used or not, it's part of our process to create and envision an ongoing life for these creatures, despite how definitive an ending to

a film may be. We had a few scenarios of what we thought the audience would next want to see in the Alien lineage and projected our own ideas of what the next *Alien* feature would be.

We weren't expecting that another element was already being added to the mix.

Predators.

Alec Gillis
Creature Effects Co-Creator
Founder: ADI

Movies are a wonderfully insidious thing. They get into your brain and take root, affecting your thoughts and actions for years. It's why my brother and I spent a summer grabbing our throats and falling backwards into the pool, like when Heston gets shot in *Planet of the Apes.* It's why we'd re-enact the skeleton fight from *Jason and the Argonauts* for hours on end (the neighbors just saw the chubby Gillis boys running around the yard with sticks…). It's why when I see the Fox logo before a movie, I still get residual chills from 1968, the summer of the *Apes.*

As a society we're all movie junkies, so what makes some of us pursue moviemaking as a career? Maybe it's because someone encouraged us, or because someone discouraged us, or simply because we didn't really think it through. In my case, by age 13, I had developed such an obsession with special effects (specifically Harryhausen's), that I could think of little else. My father was an insurance salesman who had tried to sell Dick Smith a policy, and spoke reverently about his talents, even though he chose to remain underinsured. Dad also knew that *King Kong* was only 18 inches tall, which boggled my mind. (I also learned that Kong's rampage probably wouldn't have been covered by insurance.)

These glimpses into the workings of movie magic sparked my desire to discover everything I could about the processes used in creating the images. That there was so little information available only fanned the flames of my curiosity. It was as though someone was trying to keep this world a secret, and that only the tenacious would eventually be granted this esoteric knowledge. The door cracked open a bit with an article in *Famous Monsters of Filmland* that mentioned a source for foam latex; then a call to Don Post Studios to ask about rubber cement paint, and so on. *Cinemagic* magazine was a dream come true for all Harryhausen wannabes, but every issue was a blow to the ego when you read the production reports about some kid who was doing blue screen compositing in Super-8! (Then there was the guy in Pennsylvania with the "modified aerial brace" for supporting stop motion puppets...that turned out to be Tom Woodruff, Jr.)

So, with a feeling that I was behind the curve, I set out to catch up. After a few years of ruining mom's electric eggbeaters and taking over her garage, I landed my first job on a movie. The journey began in 1980 and went like this: Roger Corman to UCLA film school to Greg Cannom to Tom Savini to Stan Winston to ADI. That makes the road seem direct and unwavering, but in reality it was fraught with uncertainty and risk. Along the way, I had the good fortune to connect with people who invested in me before there was proof that I could do what I said I could. Foremost among them is Stan Winston. I had been recommended to Stan by Jim Cameron, and based on that, Stan welcomed me into the fold without hesitation. With this level of trust, I felt comfortable taking chances in all areas of creature creating. His highly collaborative crew, consisting of Tom Woodruff Jr., Shane Mahan, John Rosengrant, Richard Landon, Shannon Shea and Rick Lazzarini, had a chemistry that really worked. Tom and I later broke off and formed ADI, but many aspects of Stan's studio continue to be a model for our own.

Nowadays there's a glut of effects films competing for audience attention, and honestly, not many of them are lucky enough to connect. Nothing would please me more than to see a couple of chubby kids playing *AVP* in their yard this summer, the summer of *AVP.*

Tom Woodruff, Jr.
Creature Effects Co-Creator
Founder: ADI

The idea behind this book was to put something into the hands of the fan that would let him see how we created the creatures for *AVP*, from design through shooting—as if we could put a camera in your hands and let you be with us every day, shooting whatever you saw. The idea behind the "artist profiles" was to give you a small glimpse of just some of the people who worked to make those creatures. Space precluded us from including everyone or providing much more than just a glimpse. In many cases you'll see the same pivotal films mentioned that influenced us in earlier days. You'll see Ray Harryhausen mentioned more than any other as a source of fascination and inspiration. Whatever the peculiar mix that got us all here, we all seem to share a passion to create characters and creatures that shock, frighten, and amaze the audience out there, that we used to be.

I grew up watching monster movies on television. It was long before DVD or even VHS (in fact, even the 8-track tape was still an invention of the future) and it was usually through sheer luck or extensive preplanning with a *TV Guide* in hand that I was able to catch a much sought-after showing of *Frankenstein* or *The Wolfman*.

Not being much for books, the only literary supplement I had was in the form of the now classic, *Famous Monsters of Filmland*. Although it rarely went into any details of how to make a monster, it was packed with stills from every monster movie ever made. Through *Famous Monsters*, I learned the names of the monster makers of the movies: Lon Chaney, Jack Pierce, Dick Smith, and Rick Baker. And I learned about John Chambers and Ray Harryhausen, my personal heroes.

As kids, I think we're drawn toward what inspires us, and we reach out for it in whatever way we can. I grew up in a small town. At the opposite side of the country, I

might just as well have been light years away from Hollywood. But I was lucky to have found such an object of focus, and luckier still to have parents who supported that interest, even if they couldn't fully understand it. With no guarantees that there was ever a future to it, they allowed me to turn my attention to my own interests—although a failing grade in fifth grade history meant boxing up the entire monster collection until I brought the grade up. They let me convert the basement of our house into a workshop and studio where I could work on my masks and my stop-motion animation.

My dad wasn't a sculptor, but he had a friend that let me borrow a mannequin head on which I could build a mask. My mom wasn't a seamstress, but she helped me make a gorilla costume. My dad wasn't a filmmaker, but he bought me a Super-8 camera for my birthday and had a friend on the police force that would let me shoot him flying his helicopter for my movie.

They both saw that spark of interest grow into that shared passion that we, as monster makers, seek to fulfill. Look, we can never be sure where we're going to end up—how the mix of influences and support and chances we take in our lives are going to come out. But for those of us whose work is in this book, the ones that got to come to work every day to make monsters for this movie, it is a dream come true.

EFFECTS PHILOSOPHY

CG or Not CG?

Every Visual Effects-driven film has an "approach" to the design of its effects. Some people call it the "effects methodology" (which sounds a bit like either a religion or a medical procedure), or the "bag of tricks" (which sounds like an amateur magic act). The phrase we prefer is the "effects philosophy". This term brings to mind images of the great Effects Philosophers sitting around on broken Doric columns asking "CG or not CG? That is the question." Okay, that's Shakespeare, who was not a philosopher, but what the heck, this is Hollywood where nobody is that literate anyway. The point is, a decision must be made as to how a film's effects are going to be accomplished.

Sometimes that decision is made during the course of the production, which leads to confusion and waste. Usually a plan, or philosophy, is arrived at well in advance so that all departments can work accordingly. One of the big philosophical questions is invariably, "Which shots are Animatronic and which are CG?"

At this point you may be expecting that we Animatronic Effects designers would step up on top of a bucket of latex and preach the evils of CG, a technique that has cut into the reliance on our traditional methods. The fact is, we love CG! That's right, we love CG...*when it is used properly*. Digital imagery is a fantastic tool that has revolutionized filmmaking. Anything from ocean storms to dinosaurs to lip-syncing dead presidents can be

accomplished with CG. Why wouldn't you use it whenever and wherever you can? Rather than answer that with a diatribe about what's wrong with CG, we instead ask the question, "Why would you use practical, on-set effects (like Animatronics) instead of CG?" Here are a few reasons:

Animatronics have presence. They are *actual* objects that exist in the same reality as the sets and the actors and are lit by the same light as the sets and the actors. They are affected by the laws of physics (gravity, momentum) and therefore are possessed of an innate realism difficult to reproduce in a graphic image. Actors respond to them more convincingly than they do to a green tennis ball on a stick. Their use in a film invariably improves the look of their CG counterparts, as they provide an exact reference for lighting and movement that the digital artist can match.

Animatronics are tactile. Because they are actually there, Animatronics can come in close contact with actors, props, and set pieces. They can drool on actors, be beaten up by actors, thrash around in water or be set on fire. None of this is impossible with a CG image, but it is expensive and difficult.

Animatronics have an aesthetic soul. It is an art whose foundation is sculpture, and sculpture has a powerful psychological impact on the viewer. Even though film is a 2-D medium, the fantastically designed human eye (connected to the even more fantastic human brain) can tell the difference

Opposite: Scar, the main Predator protagonist of *AVP*.

Above: Tom Woodruff, Jr. dons the teeth and claws once more for his third Alien film.

between an *actual* 3-D object and a graphic reproduction of a 3-D object. The other aspect of this aesthetic is one of art direction. The artists in the Animatronics world are specialists who have, in many cases, eaten, slept, and dreamt of creatures since childhood. They don't create spaceships one month, tidal waves the next, or exploding buildings after that. They make creatures. That's all they do. They're experts. And there aren't that many of them either. Visual Effects films have gotten so big (thanks largely to digital technology, which has expanded film possibilities), that CG companies have had to grow to satisfy the demand. The by-product of this growth is that a factory-approach has been adopted, sometimes leading to a soulless, generic look to the effects. This could be called the corporatization of effects. It could also be called McEffects, if one wanted to risk irking the ire of the fast food industry! (Come to think of it, fast food is what both digital and Animatronic artists have in common, given that it is our main source of sustenance during those long deadline-driven nights...and the kid's meals sometimes include cool toys of creatures we've designed.)

Above: The Predator 'Celtic' emerges from the shadows wearing one of the fourteen sets of Predator armor that ADI made for the film.

So, now that we've convinced you that Animatronics are the preferred technique of any intelligent filmmaker, you may think that we are in favor of using them whenever and wherever possible. Wrong. Animatronics, like any technique, have their limits and those limits should be taken into account when deciding where to use the technique. Generally, we wouldn't propose using a full-body Animatronic Alien to scurry along the ceiling, for instance—it would be too cumbersome to shoot, and by the end of the day the entire crew would probably hate us and we would run the risk of being removed from the crew jacket list. The rule of thumb is that you stick with the practical creature for close-ups and medium shots, and use CG for the wide shots. That's only a general rule, and *AVP* has plenty of wide shots of practical creatures where we felt we could make them work.

When we speak of using CG creatures in *AVP* we are referring mainly to the Alien Warrior or the Queen Alien, which are less human in design as compared to the Predator. This meant that the Predator was virtually always a man in a suit with an Animatronic face, unless the scene called for a particularly dangerous stunt.

All of this philosophical blabber is fine, unless the director and creative team disagree with it, in which case we are helpless to do much of anything about it, except to complain to people at bus stops and coffee shops about how "the Man is puttin' us down." Fortunately for patrons of public transportation and Denny's, Paul Anderson and the execs at Fox agreed with us even before we met with them on *AVP*. It seems that Paul is a fan of practical effects, particularly as they have been used in the *Alien* and *Predator* films. The folks at Fox had high confidence in us from our work on *Alien* [3] and *Alien Resurrection*, so we never had to make the speeches exalting the virtues of Animatronics.

This philosophy of practical effects ruling the day didn't just apply to Animatronics and performers in suits, it also extended to other areas as well. Visual Effects Supervisor John Bruno was hired to ensure that *AVP* had the level of realism that audiences have come to expect from an *Alien* or *Predator* film. John was the perfect choice for that, having been in charge of effects for films such as *True Lies*, *Cliffhanger*, and *The Abyss*, for which he won an Academy Award. One of the great things about John is that he's been around long enough to be comfortable with in-camera, practical approaches to effects. He can also nail a gopher at fifty paces, and has kept his Pasadena neighborhood gopher free for years. Both these qualifications greatly impressed the studio, and who can blame them?

John's involvement led to the decision to use even more practical effects, with some miniatures provided by Bill Pearson (Piper Maru, Weyland satellite, Piston Bullies) and other miniatures by Richard Van Den Bergh (collapsing Whaling Station, Pyramid, Queen's Chamber). John was also a big supporter of the use of a miniature Alien Queen, built by the talented folks at ADI.

It should be pointed out that while *AVP*'s effects philosophy dictated a heavy reliance on Animatronics and miniatures, that doesn't mean that there is no CG in the film. To the contrary, there are many shots of the Alien Queen relentlessly pursuing Lex or hordes of Alien Warriors, not to mention multiple airborne facehuggers eager to plant their seed in a human host. In fact, Adam Valdez, one of the best animators in the game, was in charge of bringing the digital Alien Queen to life. Adam's work can be seen in such effects orgies as *Starship Troopers* and the trilogy *Lord of the Rings*. He, along with Ben Shepherd at The Moving Picture Company in London, is responsible for the lion's share of the digital effects. It is through the hard work and dedication of talented artists on both the digital *and* Animatronic sides of the effects fence that allows the Aliens and Predators to live and do battle. The synthesis of both techniques improves

Above: Director Paul W. S. Anderson and Alien Tom Woodruff, Jr. share an interspecies discourse.

and supports the other, resulting in a more seamless and convincing experience for the viewer. The process of bringing *AVP*'s digital effects to the screen was a fascinating journey involving hundreds of hard-working artisans. It's an interesting story, but you won't read about it here. They can write their own damn book. This one is about the clay, the fiberglass, the servos, the paint, the rubber and the people who turned it all into Aliens and Predators, two of the meanest monsters ever to tear up a multiplex!

ARTIST PROFILE
YURI EVERSON
Shop Supervisor

The Pine Barrens of New Jersey didn't offer little Yuri much to capture his interest. Although his father Roy was a fine art painter, the only color young Yuri was interested in was red; blood red. During the 1980's horror movie boom, he was thrilled by the work of John Carpenter and make-up artists Rick Baker and Rob Bottin. Zombies and crazed killers took over his imagination, along with Carpenter's *The Thing*. After two years in film school in New York, he couldn't stand it any longer. He packed up and went to L.A. to make his gruesome dreams come true. Greg Cannom gave him his first break, which led to a stint at Rick Baker's on *Gremlins II*. "Rick runs a highly professional shop, and that made a big impression

on me", Yuri says with admiration. In 1990 Yuri was hired at ADI as a sculptor for *Point Break,* and has been here since, as ADI's longest-employed staffer. In the 40 projects since he started, the company has grown into one of the most respected in the field, and Yuri has gone from one of the crew to the head of the crew. His job is multi-faceted. There's scheduling, hiring, coordinating, and settling inevitable personality conflicts. On set his duties extend into puppeteering, make-up application, arranging the next day's work, and rigging gags. If Tom and Alec are unavailable to be on set, Yuri takes charge of the ADI crew. For instance, he managed a good portion of the set work for *Starship Troopers*, and all of it on *Bubble Boy*. His depth of experience gives us the freedom to focus on concept design, art direction, and performance issues. His artistic abilities, resourcefulness, and knowledge of materials provide valuable consistency as

we seek to improve techniques with each project. How does he feel about his work? In his words, "Through ADI, I've been all over the world, met some amazing people and learned the art and the business, and how to manage them both. For that I'm eternally grateful." Yuri's dad passed away, but not before seeing his son's success in the movies. He also cites his mother, Patricia, as a main source of support, along with his wife Melissa and their two sons Ethan and Owen.

DESIGN

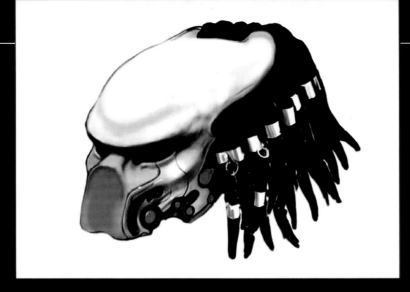

To The Drawing Board...

O n July 1, 2003, we officially began work on AVP. We say "officially" because that was the day the first payment check cleared. We [h]ad actually begun organizing and scheduling ear[li]er, but these are things we didn't want the studio [to] know, or we'd appear over-anxious. We kept a [co]ol exterior and pretended to be jaded pros, but [b]ack at ADI the mood was giddy. After all, we were [b]uilding two of the greatest modern monster-movie [ic]ons, and the buzz on the Internet was electric, [th]ough not all positive. We felt a great responsibili[t]y to the fans to do these beloved characters jus[ti]ce. The build list was daunting. With the multiple [P]redator and Alien characters, there were over thir[t]y full-body suits to be created, including fourteen [fu]ll sets of Predator armor, and seven servo-artic[u]lated heads between them. Five hand-pup[p]eted facehuggers, six floppy facehug[g]ers, one fully articulated Anima[tr]onic facehugger, and several [c]hestbursters were to be [b]uilt. There was Predator [w]eaponry, some of it [m]echanical, as well [a]s a completely

hydraulic, computer-controlled Alien Warrior required. Also needed were ten articulated eggs and another twenty positionable ones. There were Alien tails and faces that could be sliced in battle, exploding Aliens, stunt dummies of Predators and Aliens, several miniature queens... and of course, the Mother of all Aliens, a full size hydraulic, motion-controlled Queen Alien!

When compared to the previous Alien or Predator films, AVP had more work than any of them combined. We estimated that we would need nine months to accomplish this enormous task.

Opposite: Although some variations were made during the sculpting stage, this drawing by Farzad Varahramyan and Joe Pepe provided most of the information regarding the look of the Predator armor.

Top: Concept art for a Predator helmet by Carlos Huante.

Bottom: A design sketch by Farzad Varahramyan for an updated Predator gauntlet housing those infamous wrist blades.

What we didn't stop to consider was that this was a *summer movie*, which meant that in order to meet the release date, all the work had to be completed in FIVE MONTHS! After working on three *Alien* movies, we just couldn't stand the thought of someone else at the helm, and we looked forward to creating a new Predator. This was not a project to pass up.

Our first meeting with Paul Anderson did much to set our minds at ease. Having worked with him on *Mortal Kombat*, we already had a great relationship, and how could you not? Paul's love of movies and moviemaking was refreshing and his vision for the film was big and bold. He also understood our time limits and helped shape a workload that was very specific to his script's needs. There simply wasn't time to build unnecessary pieces, and he knew exactly what he needed and what he didn't. Fortunately, Paul loved the Alien as we had realized it for *Alien Resurrection*, but asked for a few changes. Per his request, we made the spindly hands of the Alien into meatier, longer-taloned weapons that looked more formidable next to the Predator. Paul also wanted a color scheme that skewed more to the blacks and metallics than the sepia tones of the previous films. With these modifications, we then were able to use existing molds of the Alien Warrior.

The Queen, however, was completely recreated from the ground up. In *Aliens*, she was a full-scale character with partial Animatronic functions (head and face). Two stunt men lying in her torso provided her arm movement. Pretty cool for 1986, but Paul's script demanded much more specific action, and advancements in Animatronics demanded that we bring her into the new millennium. This time around she needed a sleek silhouette, combined with speed and performability that was previously impossible.

Luckily, producers Tom Hammel and Chris Symes planned the film so that the Queen's first day of shooting was a month into the schedule, which gave us a total of five months to create her, start to finish. Not much time, but at this point in our company's history, we've become adept at doing the undoable.

The Predators were a different challenge, as there were no previous molds upon which to base the new iterations. We were working at Stan Winston's when *Predator* was made, but we had very little to do with it, as we were concentrating on another Stan Winston project, *Monster Squad*. We occasionally looked over Stan's shoulder as he designed the Predator, and lent moral support to Steve Wang, Matt Rose, and Shannon Shea, who

Above: Early Predator armor concept art by Farzad Varahramyan. Because the story is set in Antarctica and the Predators were going to be pitted against Aliens, a potentially fiercer foe than us humans, the design mandate called for heavier armor and more extensive body coverage.

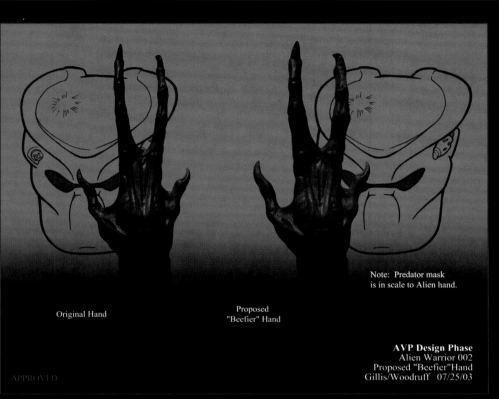

Original Hand

Proposed
"Beefier" Hand

Note: Predator mask
is in scale to Alien hand.

AVP Design Phase
Alien Warrior 002
Proposed "Beefier"Hand
Gillis/Woodruff 07/25/03

APPROVED

Left: The case of the Warrior Alien's hands is one example of how ADI uses the computer as a design tool. Because Director Paul W. S. Anderson feared the existing style of hands might appear a bit weak and flimsy when interacting with the gargantuan Predators, he wanted the hands to be "beefed up" a little. Photos of the existing hands were manipulated digitally using Photoshop to pre-visualize these requests. Once the artwork had been approved, sculptures of the hands were altered accordingly.

Below: Alec Gillis, Tom Woodruff, Jr., and designer Joe Pepe discuss the latest stack of concept drawings.

were the key guys on that project. Beyond that, we were merely fans of the movie, like everybody else. As with our experience on the *Alien* films, we felt a tremendous responsibility to treat the re-creation of this revered character with the respect it deserved. Also, Stan Winston, who we consider to be our mentor, wouldn't let us live it down if we blew it!

The design challenges for the Predators stemmed from both function and character. In this film the Predators would be engaging in ritual combat not with humans, but with Aliens. This meant that they would need more protective armor than previously seen. This new armor needed to retain the aesthetic of the Predator culture we'd seen before but extrapolated to full body coverage. Just what is the Predator aesthetic? The first film showed us a mix of Asian and tribal influence along with a rough-hewn primitive quality to the body armor. *Predator 2* introduced a more ornate, almost insect-like look. Our job was to turn these eclectic motifs into a unified aesthetic. The Predator society builds sophisticated spaceships, yet they should not look as sleek and hi-tech as a *Star Wars* Stormtrooper. They are a tribal culture, yet their look should not be as primitive as the Orcs from *Lord of the Rings*. They are also a warrior culture, so the ornate cannot conflict with the practical. Huge samurai-style decorative projections could be a disadvantage in a fight with an Alien, for instance.

The Predator weapons were refined this time, as well. The spear became sleeker and more

elegant. The throwing disc changed into a deadly multi-bladed, collapsible buzz saw. The good old twin wrist blades were given a face-lift, and made longer. One Predator, dubbed "Chopper," has large scimitar-like forearm blades, another a reworked net gun. Five helmets of new design were created, although "Scar," the main Predator, wears one similar to the original.

This film owes as much to the Dark Horse comic series as it does its cinematic predecessors. In keeping with that, we decided that the Predators themselves should reflect a comic book-style silhouette, possessing more heroic proportions: wider shoulders, narrower waists, smaller heads. We also

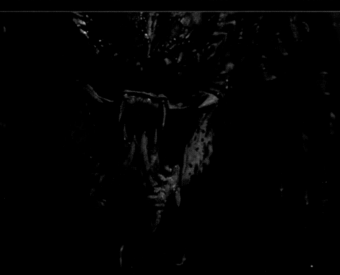

lengthened their dreadlocks to help punctuate head movement. Other changes were script-driven. Because Scar teams up with the film's heroine, Lex, we thought of him as a romantic leading man. Okay, there was really no intergalactic, interspecies romance going on here, but the subtext was there, at least in our twisted minds. This Predator was not here strictly for scares as before, but as an actual *character*! He was to spend more time without his armor mask, and needed to convey emotions such as rage, respect, pain, surprise, and even a bit of sadness. As Paul Anderson conceived him, this Predator wasn't a monster, he was an actor (nothing draws us to a project like the opportunity to create a rounded character). With that in mind, he became sculpturally more regal (dare we say it: *handsome*?) and in color scheme, we opted for less pale, clammy amphibian tones and more human skin tones. His eyes were based on a predatory cat's, and imbued with warm golden tones and a slightly larger iris. Finally, we reduced the amount of slime coating of prior incarnations, deeming that more of a trademark of the Alien than the Predator.

Ironically, all of this thought and effort is intended to go unnoticed by the audience. The last thing we want is for fans to think that we've ruined one of their favorite monsters in an effort to improve it. What we hope for is that they *feel* the changes. If we've done our job, the viewer will unconsciously sense a greater realism and expressiveness of performance, and a tightening of design. Stan Winston's and H.R.Giger's original designs were groundbreaking, but with each new film and new director comes new requirements and new design modifications. It's a tricky path to tread; on the one hand we don't want a rote duplication of what has gone before, then again, change for the sake of change is pointless. While we may never recapture the surprise and freshness of those moments in the first films when the world was initially exposed to these now classic creatures, *AVP* provided the opportunity to subtly develop them and take them in new directions.

Top: The extra-terrestrial trophy hunter who was introduced in John McTiernan's 1987 film, *Predator*.

Bottom: Another Predator pays Earth a visit in 1990's *Predator 2*.

Opposite: Scar, the main Predator featured in *AVP* (played by Ian Whyte). Because the audience had to come to respect and empathize with him, subtle changes were made to his facial anatomy to make him more heroic.

01 This concept art of the Queen Alien with her egg sac is another example of digital and traditional media being combined to efficiently communicate an idea. Chris Ayers cut up and reassembled a photograph of the Queen sculpture in the computer to assume the appropriate pose and then added a traditionally-drawn egg sac.

02 This sketch by R.K. Post is an example of one of the early challenges tackled by the design team: imagining how Lex, the story's heroine, might use pieces of an Alien exoskeleton as armor. This idea was eventually streamlined to include only a shield and spear made from an Alien head and tail.

03 While exploring possibilities for the Queen Alien's restraints, Farzad Varahramyan toyed around with the idea of a double bit, one for each of her nasty mouths.

04 When an original prop of a calcified facehugger, beautifully aged by Dave Selvadurai, was deemed still too pristine, Chris Ayers deteriorated it further via Photoshop.

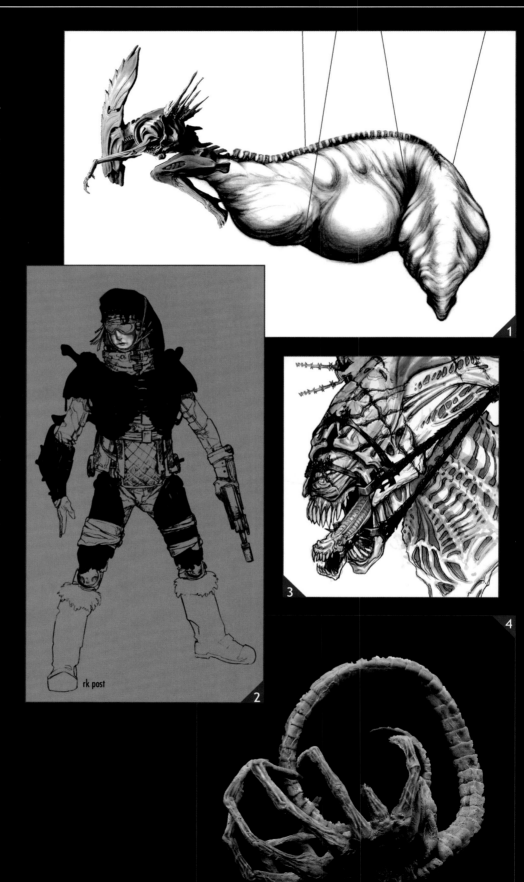

AVP DESIGN PHASE
GRID 004
GILLIS/WOODRUFF 08/14/03

05 Photoshop concept art of "Grid" by Chris Ayers. The size and pattern of the Predator's metallic net which cuts into Grid's carapace, as well as what would be an appropriate amount of oozing acid blood, all had to be determined in the design phase.

06 Joe Pepe had to put himself in an Alien's head, quite literally, when he did concept sketches of a warrior brain.

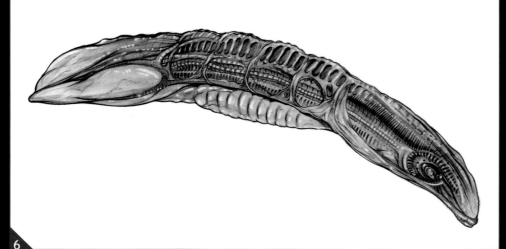

01 Concept art of the Alien Queen in her egg-harvesting restraints by Farzad Varahramyan. Because of time and budgetary considerations, this would ultimately be realized as a quarter-scale miniature instead of a full-size set.

02 Early in the design process, it was decided that some artistic license could be taken with the queen. Experimenting with loose maquettes, Akihito Ikeda added various spikes and other forms to her carapace. The final design, shown at bottom, featured subtle yet distinctive changes from the queens in previous films.

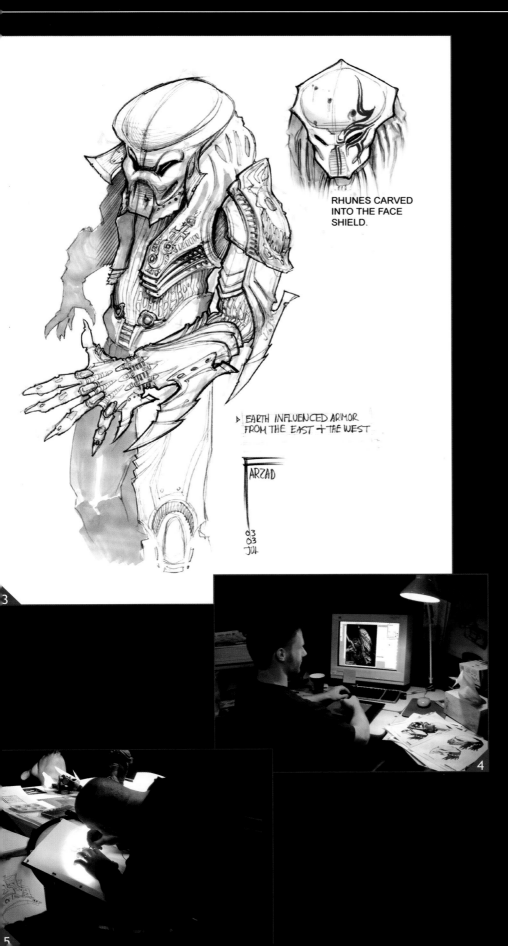

RHUNES CARVED
INTO THE FACE
SHIELD.

▷ EARTH INFLUENCED ARMOR
FROM THE EAST + THE WEST

FARZAD

03
03
JUL

03 Director Paul W. S. Anderson wanted the Predators of *AVP* to employ slight variations of weaponry that had already been introduced to audiences, but also to feature some brand new instruments of carnage. This drawing, by Farzad Varah-ramyan, depicts a blade extending laterally from the forearm which later evolved into a telescoping 3-foot-long scimitar blade featured in the final film.

04-05 From pencils to pixels, the members of ADI's *AVP* design team (including Joe Pepe, left, and Chris Ayers, right) used a wide variety of media to translate their ideas to a visual form.

3

4

5

01 Small-scale, loose sculptural studies called maquettes (such as this one by Don Lanning) are a good way to quickly explore a wide spectrum of design possibilities. This particular maquette is a good example of the somewhat exaggerated comic book proportions and "heroic feel" that director Paul W. S. Anderson requested.

02 Intricate detail, as in this drawing by R.K. Post, can initiate a healthy creative dialogue between the director and design team as they slowly converge on a character's visual identity.

03 A good concept drawing conveys not only what a character, vehicle, or environment *looks* like, but also personality and emotion. The Predator's strength and no-nonsense attitude comes across in this study by Carlos Huante.

1

ARTIST PROFILE

CARLOS HUANTE
Concept Artist

Carlos was always an artist, drawing all the time. High school art classes and drawing classes at Art Center and The California Art Institute helped shape his talents but it was the "bloodbath of learning from professional criticism" that kept him on his toes. Every Ray Harryhausen film, as well as *King Kong, Star Wars*, and *Alien* were all inspiring to this plucky youngster. It has been a treat in the past to have him on *Wolf, Jumanji, Mortal Kombat,* and *Alien Resurrection*. On *AVP*, Carlos enjoyed the change of pace of designing weapons and Predator helmets as he spends most of his time designing living creatures. He recently put out a book presenting some of his fascinating art, *Monstruo – The Art of Carlos Huante*.

FARZAD VARAHRAMYAN
Concept Artist

Like many kids, Farzad's imagination was sparked the first time he saw *Star Wars.* Joe Johnston and Ralph McQuarrie's illustrations inspired him to attend Art Center College of Design. Farzad was discovered by ADI (it's easy to "discover" someone as talented as this!), and he started his first movie job, *Jumanji*. The film was directed by his idol, Joe Johnston, which explains why all his designs were drenched in nervous sweat. Farzad says: "It was a thrill to be associated with *AVP* and the two worlds it united. I had the opportunity to contribute to both the Predator design as well as one of my all time favorites, the Queen Alien!" For Farzad, more fun than working on the movies is sharing them with his wife Vera, son Maxwell, and daughter, Isabella.

01 Depending on a film's budget and pre-production schedule, anywhere from tens to hundreds of designs can be created for a single prop or character. This final design for Scar's ceremonial dagger by Joe Pepe was arrived at only after exploring many different directions.

02 An early ceremonial dagger design by R.K. Post.

03 Final artwork for the Predator's wrist blades by Joe Pepe. In the director's effort to "up the ante" in *AVP*, the wrist blades were made to extend much further than in the previous Predator films.

04 When Joe Pepe designed a multitude of different-sized Predator shoulder cannons as called for in the script, he paid close attention to the previously-established design aesthetic of the original cannon and deviated from this only with strategic care.

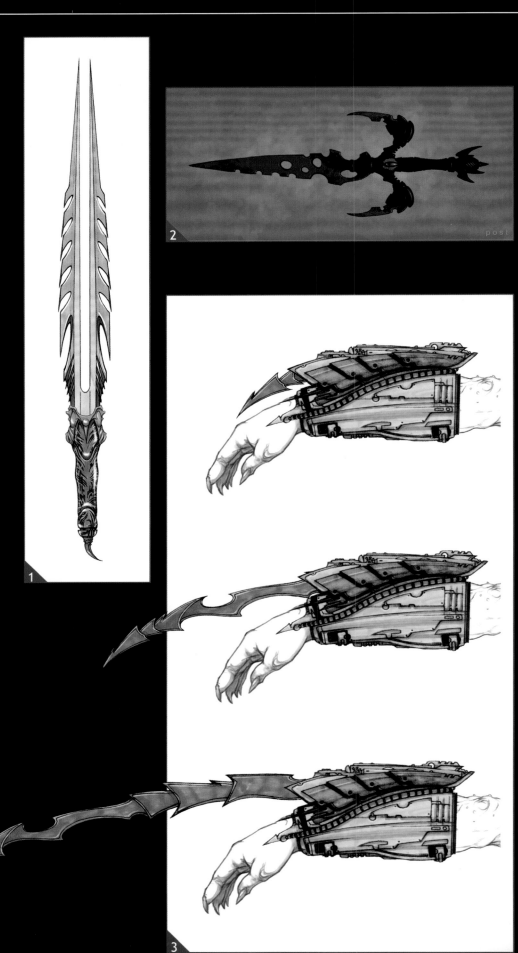

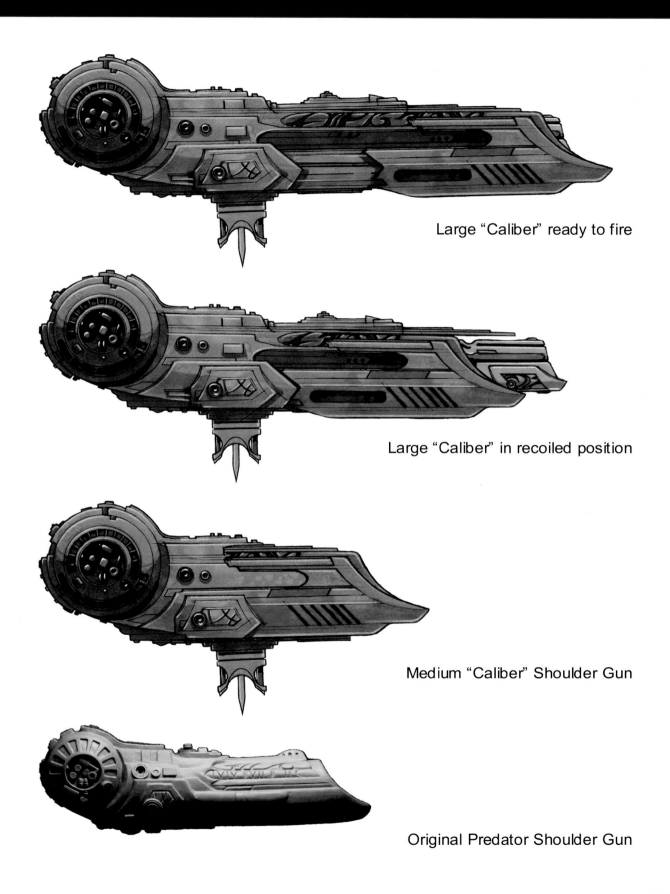

Large "Caliber" ready to fire

Large "Caliber" in recoiled position

Medium "Caliber" Shoulder Gun

Original Predator Shoulder Gun

1 Final approved artwork of the Predator net gun by Joe Pepe. The alien, who is snared by its projectile netting and would come to be known as "Grid", would have preferred it if this item had stayed on the drawing board.

2 Joe Pepe's concept art of the Predator gauntlet showing the underside of the wrist computer lid.

3 An early variation on a shoulder cannon by Farzad Varahramyan.

4-07 In order to help the audience differentiate between the multiple Predator characters featured in the script, it was decided that each Predator would have a distinctive helmet. From top to bottom, helmet concepts by Carlos Huante (top two), Chris Ayers, and Farzad Varahramyan.

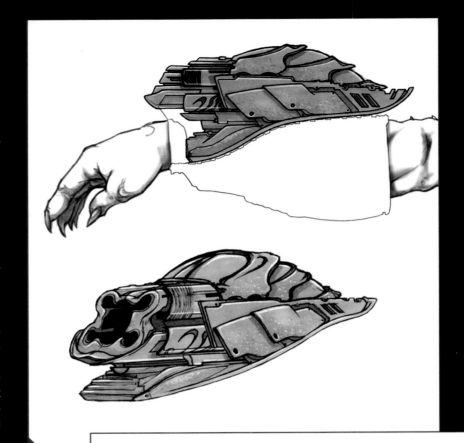

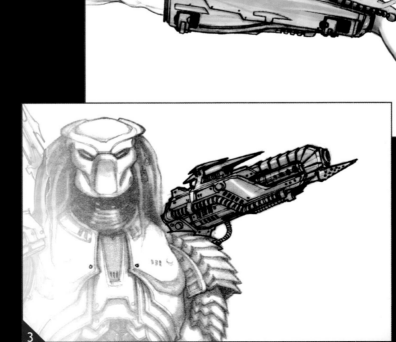

JOSEPH PEPE
Concept Artist

Joe began drawing at the age of four. Growing up in a very creative and talented family, he spent much of his time in museums and visiting art studios. After seeing *Star Wars* and *Alien*, Joe's career objective was set! Accepting a scholarship from the prestigious Pratt Institute in Brooklyn and graduating with honors, Joe also completed an internship at Disney Feature Animation in Florida. The next decade was spent as a Visual Effects Animation Artist/Designer with Disney. A friend introduced him to Alec Gillis who granted him the opportunity to work on *AVP* alongside the artists he had admired for so many years! Joe is a freelance artist, collaborating with his wife, Kimberly L. O'Donnell, and his brothers on film and television projects in L.A.

CHRIS AYERS
Concept Artist

Age 2: Imprinted on *Star Wars*.
Age 4: Could tell you whether a dromedary has one hump or two.
Age 6: Exasperated his parents by requesting Bill Peet's *Whingdingdilly* every night for the bedtime story.
Age 10: Relentlessly begged his sister to reenact the skeleton battle from *Jason & the Argonauts* with him.
Age 16: Coaxed out of bed each day by the promise of a new *Calvin & Hobbes* in the morning paper.
Age 20: Introduced to the Renaissance firsthand while studying art in Florence.
Age 24: Moved west from Minnesota to draw some monsters and "bought" his way into the film industry by bidding on a tour of ADI at a fundraising auction.

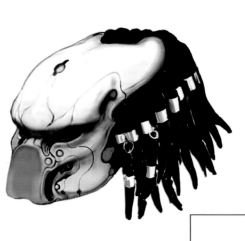

4

5

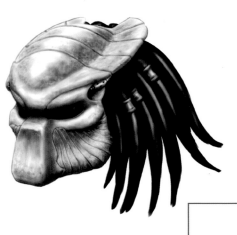

6

7

01 When designing the Predator Elders who appear later in the film, Photoshop was used to "finish" a partially-completed Elder sculpture. Facial scarring, bone-shard piercings, and larger, engraved mandible tusks were added digitally. Because of the film's extremely short build schedule, the ability to quickly show the director several variations on a theme before committing to clay was essential to meeting the deadlines. Sculptural elements by Andy Schoneberg and Bruce Spaulding Fuller. Photoshop work by Chris Ayers.

02 Concept art by Joe Pepe for the Predator's shuriken, or throwing disc. The size, shape, and number of blades, as well as the design of the case, went through many variations before being settled upon.

Opposite: One mother of a migraine; Farzad Varahramyan's lavishly-rendered depiction of the queen after her carapace is severely damaged by a Predator wrist bomb.

PREDATOR ELDER (REVISED)
• More scarring added
• Head rings removed on one side
• Remaining head rings changed to bone shards
• Deeper carving on mandible tusks

AVP DESIGN PHASE
PREDATOR ELDER 003
GILLIS/WOODRUFF   10/09/03

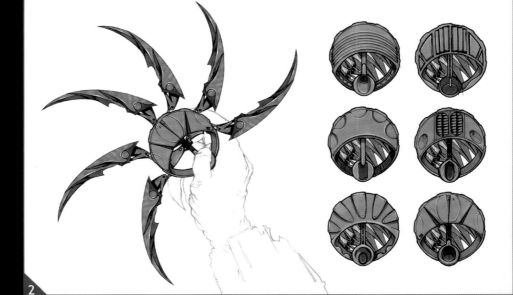

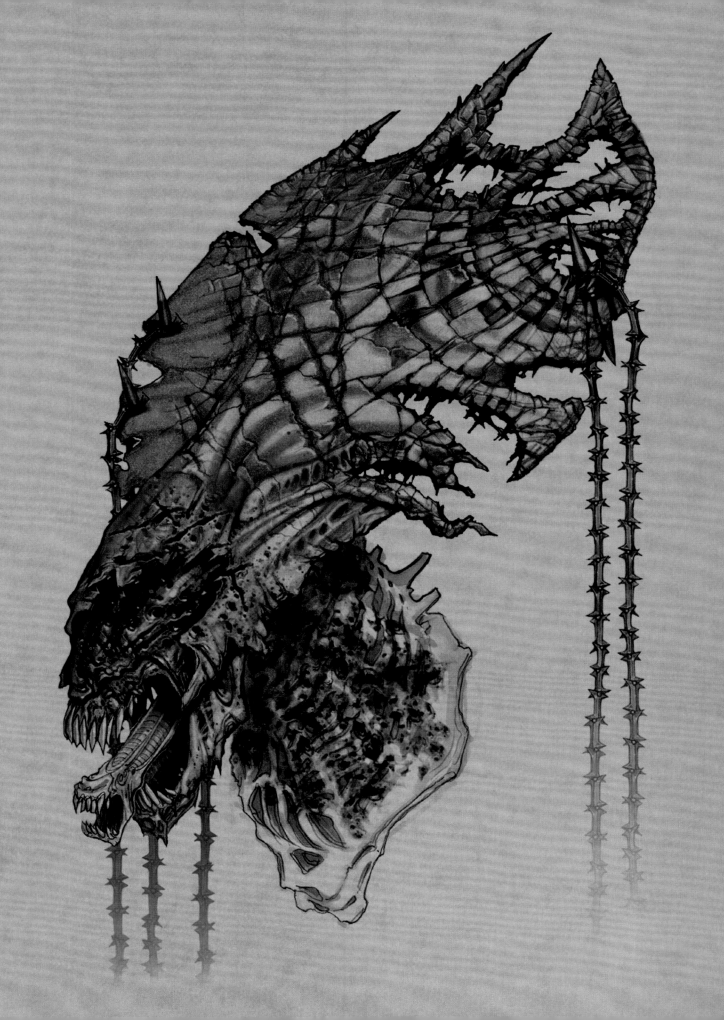

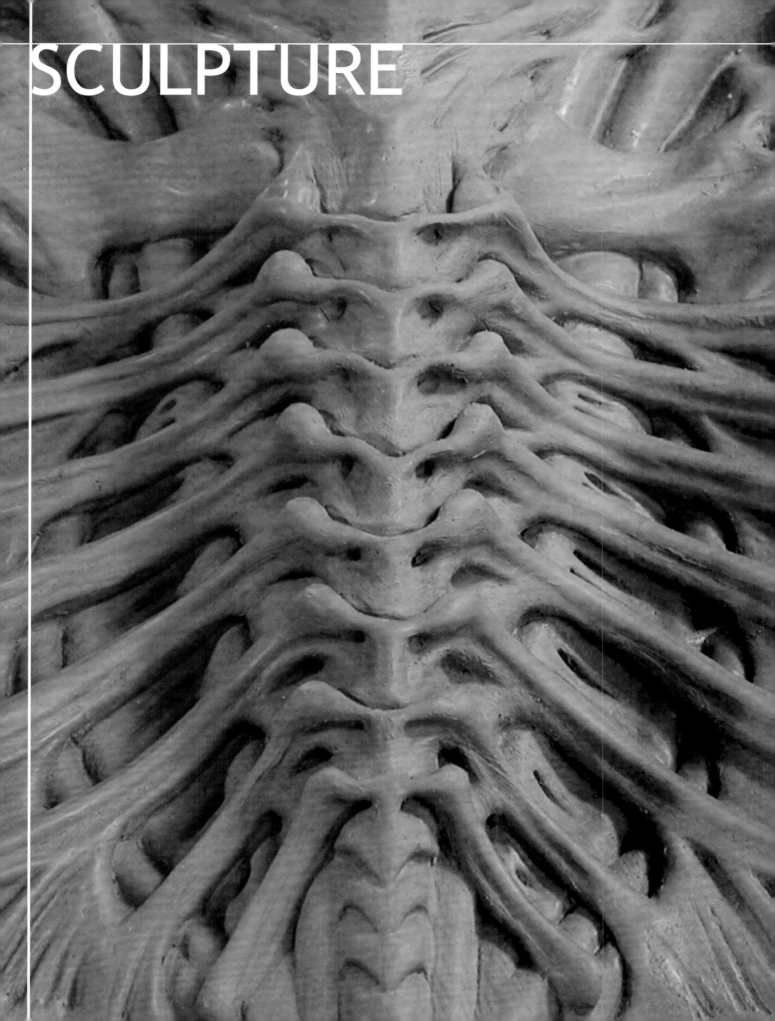

SCULPTURE

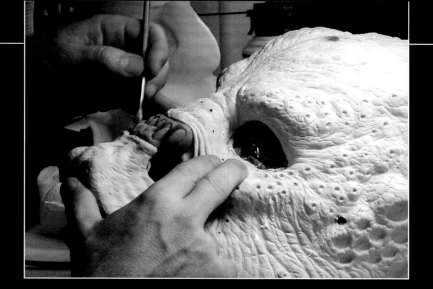

From Clay Comes Form

Sculpture is in many ways the foundation of Animatronics. It is the point where the discussions, the plans, and the drawings actually become real. Two-dimensional designing is a critical first step, but nothing's really tangible until sculpture starts. That's when you find out if the concepts you've been pursuing on paper are going to work, or be relegated to the dung heap. There's a misconception that sculptors are not designers, especially when a team of sketch artists have produced illustrations on paper. The fact is that no 2-D art is a complete design. The interpretation of flat art to sculpture is an artistic process that can be likened to acting: the words are written, but they live or die by the artist who breathes life into them. The good illustrator knows how to put a workable design on paper and the good sculptor knows how to pull the essence of the design off that paper. When both designers are at that level, the results can be thrilling. On *AVP* we were fortunate to have not only many of our tried and true artists, but some terrific new additions as well.

One of the challenges to an Animatronics or make-up sculptor is working "neutral." Artists often seek to heighten the impact of a piece by adding an expressive gesture or action pose. Since our sculptures will ultimately be capable of real movement (as suits, Animatronics, or Make-ups) there is no need to imply movement in the clay form. The sculptor must also take into account the next steps in the process; mold-making and mechanization. Coordination with mold-makers and mechanical designers can drive a sculptor insane if he's not used to taking input. But the greatest challenge to a sculptor is taking input from us—we can really nitpick! It's because we view this step with a critical eye, and we love working with sculptors who find collaboration rewarding. There are many talented people who do brilliant work on their own, but the work done under our roof must satisfy the demands of the art direction, the script, and the schedule, which is why we give very focused and specific direction to all of our artists. For us there's nothing more exciting than directing a group of talented people toward a common artistic goal. We usually find that when given the proper parameters, artists will exceed both our expectations as well as their own.

On a technical level, we used many different materials to realize the sculptures on *AVP*. Larger - scale sculptures tended to be worked out in water-based clays, while many others were non-drying oil-based clays. The first Queen sculpture completed was the quarter-scale miniature, which was scanned and output to a full-scale rigid foam copy. That form was then given a further "punching up" of detail. A third-scale wax version was also made from that scan, and was detailed similarly.

Opposite: Fine sculptural details like the underside of this quarter-scale queen carapace will often be obscured on film by shadows, slime, or frenzied motion, only to to be seen on the pages of books like this. It attests, however, to the discipline and care that is taken by these artists to make their creations as realistic as possible.
Above: Andy Schoneberg sculpts a new set of Predator chompers. *AVP*'s Predators have four additional upper teeth compared to the original,

Above: Mike O'Brien details a new back appendage for the Alien Warriors, one of the few changes made to them for *AVP*.

The Predator weapons were largely forms built by hand out of plastics and then molded for duplication. Sculptural details, which adorned knife or spear handles, were incorporated into the patterns to add a touch of Predator aesthetic. *AVP* required a wide range of sculptural tasks, each with a specific style. The organic look of the Predators, the "Giger-esque" style of the Queen, the primitive elegance of the Predator technology; all combined with a rigorous work pace that required some of the best sculptors in the industry. Fortunately for us, most Animatronics sculptors have dreamed of working on *AVP* for as long as the fans have been waiting to see the film.

Above: Though it was eventually cut, a planned miniature scene featuring naked Predators rising from a suspended-animation-inducing pool of goo required the creation of an anatomically-correct third-scale Predator.

Above: Bruce Spaulding Fuller and Don Lanning sculpt the Predator body. For the original *Predator*, much of the armor was incorporated into the same sculpture as the flesh. *AVP* required a different approach because at one point the script called for scenes with unarmored Predators. Also, having the armor as separate pieces provided more wardrobe options when outfitting the different Predator characters.

Right: Tom Woodruff, Jr., Sculpting Supervisor Andy Schoneberg, Shop Supervisor Yuri Everson, and Alec Gillis discuss the progress of two queen head sculptures, one quarter-scale and one full-scale.

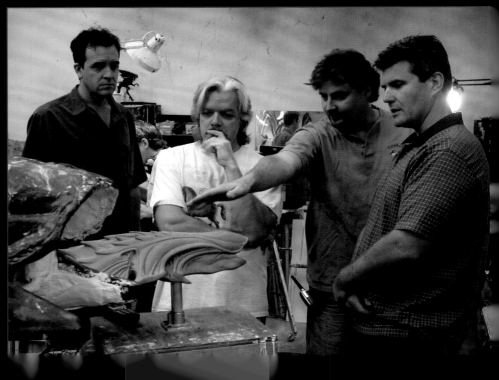

1 How many sculptors does it take to screw in a…? Oh, wait a minute. Mike O'Brien, Andy Schoneberg, Steve Koch, and Dave Selvadurai work on various assignments in the ADI Sculpting Department.

2 A front view of the finished quarter-scale Alien Queen torso.

3 The finished quarter-scale queen sculpture. This image was submitted to the director for final approval on proportion, posture, and detailing.

4 Akihito Ikeda works on the quarter-scale queen torso. Although based on the original queen from *Aliens*, she was given a thinner waist and changes were made to the surface detail.

5 Finished view of the quarter-scale queen head carapace. The added spiny structures match her prickly personality.

6 Teeth made of Super Sculpey were pressed into the clay head of the quarter-scale queen.

7 Akihito Ikeda works on the quarter-scale queen carapace, adding great levels of detail to the entire surface, including the underside, which most likely will never be seen in the final film.

AVP DESIGN PHASE
QUEEN 045
GILLIS/WOODRUFF 08/18/03

ANDY SCHONEBERG
Sculpting Department Head

Andy's list of credits with ADI is as long as his hair used to be. Some of the highlights (film, not hair) are: *Demolition Man*, *Wolf*, *The Santa Clause 1 & 2*, *Mortal Kombat*, *Jumanji*, *Tremors II*, *The X-Files Movie*, *Alien Resurrection*, *Bedazzled*, and *Hollow Man*.

Hailing from Montana, Andy's early influences were the works of Dick Smith and John Chambers, but it wasn't until he saw a copy of Richard Corson's Stage Make-up book that his brain began to squirm and he decided he would expire if he didn't get into the movie business. Andy has no formal make-up training, but he gorged on art classes in high school and college, excelling in drawing, painting, design, sculpture and calligraphy. He was also one of the original 100 students of Dick Smith's make-up course.

As ADI's key sculptor on *AVP*, Andy is most proud of his work on the Queen Alien, adding a new level of grace and refinement to the character that we hope fans will appreciate.

Andy has two teenage daughters, Emily and Elise, and is engaged to ADI Production Coordinator, Nicole Michaud. Until reading this book, none of them realized that Andy is a recovered mime (as if calligraphy isn't bad enough).

01 The approved sculpture of the quarter-scale queen body was cyber-scanned and enlarged to a rough full-scale foam sculpture by a computerized milling machine. Using a casting of the quarter-scale sculpt as reference, Andy Schoneberg and Dave Selvadurai clean up and detail the full-size piece.

02 Andy Schoneberg details the back of the full-size queen sculpture.

03 Tim Martin finesses a clay skyscraper into the queen's detailed tongue.

04 Before it is turned over to the molding department Mike O'Brien makes some last-minute refinements to the queen body. The foam has been painted to seal it for the molding process.

05 Sculpture of the "battle-damaged" queen head which results after she gets a little too close for comfort to a Predator wrist bomb.

06 Another view of the fractured queen carapace shows the further extent of the damage.

07 One of the queen's six back spines.

08 Reverse angle of the back spine.

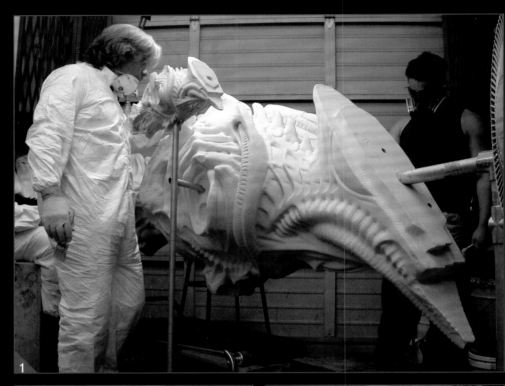

1

2

3

4

5

6

7

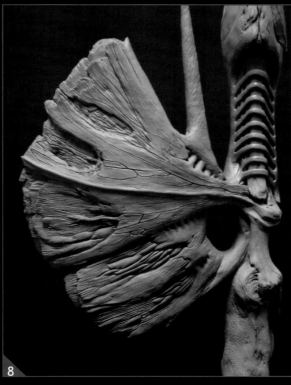

8

ARTIST PROFILE

AKIHITO IKEDA
Sculptor

Already an accomplished make-up effects artist in his native Japan, Aki was able to work at ADI on *AVP* through a specialized internship. A fan of the earlier *Alien* films, his early inspiration also came from artists like Jimi Onisi and Picasso. His mastery of sculpture included the ability to be both very precise and fast in turning design sketches into real forms. Through his company, Shiniseya, Aki exercises his visual sense and concept abilities in the make-up fashion world as well, assisted by his beautiful wife, Atsuko.

MIKE O'BRIEN
Sculptor

This New Yorker couldn't have escaped becoming a monster maker if he'd tried. His first artistic influences were his mom's paintings of Barnabas Collins and Frankenstein (Mike's mom has got it goin' on!), and his dad's custom-built choppers. He started sculpting after becoming frustrated by the lack of quality in a store-bought Freddy Krueger mask. He was the most popular kid on the block each Halloween with his own Haunted House, which provided great experience that helped land a job in the movies. *AVP* is Mike's first credit as an ADI sculptor, and as an Alien and Predator fan, it was a dream come true. He's especially proud of his work on the new Queen Alien, and is currently busy promoting his model kit company, Mob Scene.

01 To meet the short build deadline, the sculpting process was expedited by using a casting of the queen head from *Alien Resurrection* instead of starting completely from scratch. Here Dave Selvadurai adds clay to the casting to incorporate modifications that were first designed on a small-scale maquette.

02 Tom Woodruff points out the queen's only ticklish spot to Jeff Buccacio and Alec Gillis.

03 Akihito Ikeda works on detailing the quarter-scale queen head (foreground) while Dave Selvadurai echoes his sculpting strokes, but at a much greater magnitude (midground) on the full-size queen. Meanwhile, Bruce Spaulding Fuller (background) starts to rough out shapes for a Predator backpack.

04 A close-up view of the third-scale queen's bomb-scarred head carapace.

05 In addition to a quarter-scale and a full-scale queen, ADI also constructed a third-scale queen puppet. Rather than starting from scratch, and since the quarter-scale sculpture had already been cyberscanned to help with the full-size queen, a third-scale head was output in hard wax via a computerized milling machine. Although the wax copy faithfully reproduced much of the original detail, a pass of hand-tooling was required to make it a perfect match. Constantly referring to the original quarter-scale clay sculpture (brown) for accuracy, Steve Koch works on refining the third-scale wax copy (gray).

6

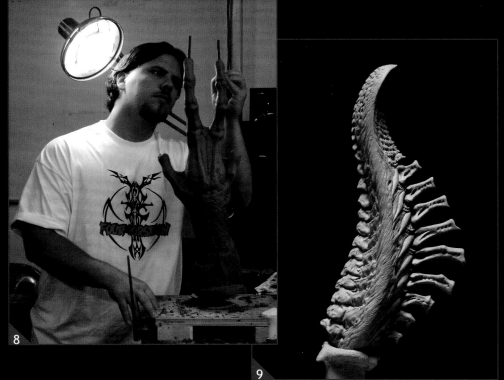

7

8

9

06 For a scene in which the Predator Scar kills and then methodically carves up a warrior, ADI needed to produce an Alien brain. Though the scene was brief, a great deal of time was given to creating a hybrid of organically and mechanically-influenced forms that echoed H.R. Giger's design aesthetic of the original *Alien*.

07 Andy Schoneberg ensures symmetry (and avoids loneliness) by using a mirror as he sculpts an Alien chestburster.

08 In order to appear more menacing while battling the Predators, Director Paul W. S. Anderson requested the hands of the Alien Warriors be "beefed up." Pete Farrell "beefs" as only Pete Farrell can.

09 Final sculpture of the warrior back appendage, a new addition for the Aliens of *AVP*.

1 The quarter-scale sculpture of the Alien Queen's egg sac began as a small 8-inch maquette which was sliced into cross-sections. Traced outlines of these cross-sections were enlarged via the computer and used as stencils for a plywood infrastructure. Here, Steve Koch attaches chicken wire to the form to define a rough mass.

2 The finished quarter-scale egg sac sculpture with a similarly-scaled egg for size reference.

3 Top view of the finished egg sac.

4 Alec Gillis demonstrates to Steve Koch the correct intergalactic technique for taking an Alien Queen's temperature.

5 Model-making Supervisor Nick Seldon, Alec Gillis, and Mechanical Supervisor Dave Penikas confer over the Predator's extendable wrist blades. Constant communication between departments throughout the design and fabrication processes is essential to avoid logistical problems down the road.

6 Mad mad modeler Nick Seldon busy at work on a variety of Predator weapons. Look carefully and you can see unfinished parts, prototypes, and plans for the ceremonial dagger, the shuriken, the wrist computer, and the large shoulder cannon.

7 Using full-size artwork from the ADI Art Department as a guide, Erik Stohl creates a Predator wrist blade.

8 David Chamberlain details a Predator scimitar blade.

NICK SELDON
Model Maker

Nick has been in the effects industry for over 20 years, but this is his first experience at ADI. As an accomplished miniature builder, he hasn't overlapped much into the world of creatures. The irony is, like many of us, his first inspirations were the films of creature maestro, Ray Harryhausen. "While I was working away on the Shuriken, I overheard one of the sculptors talking enthusiastically about Harryhausen! This was noteworthy, because it's usually me who brings up his name." Nick enjoys chatting about his idol, and we all listen...especially when he's holding a Predator weapon!

STEVE KOCH
Sculptor

At ten, Steve was making his own movies, following the influences of Willis O'Brien and Ray Harryhausen. After high school in N.Y., he enrolled at USC, also supplying effects for other students. By the late 80's, Steve was producing miniatures and effects for clients such as The Disney Channel, McDonalds, and Lego. As a freelance painter, he met his future wife, Carol (an accomplished artist herself), but wanted to work on bigger projects. Luckily, we were the first big shop to see his portfolio and hire him (it helps to be listed alphabetically). *AVP* is his eleventh film for ADI. Steve's also served as VFX Art Director on the *Austin Powers* movies and is currently working on a stop-motion film project of his own.

01 The finished sculpture of Scar, minus his mandibles which were sculpted as a separate piece to accommodate the Animatronic components that would later be inserted into them.

02 A back view of Scar's head reveals the numerous placement holes where 66 dreadlocks would be added later to the final skins.

03 The Predator Elders were based on the "hero" Scar sculpture and modified (such as a stronger and more furrowed brow and larger teeth). The metal rings were just a quick concept idea for some interesting tribal markings, but were ultimately never used.

04 A rear view of the finely textured full-size Predator body.

05 Bruce Spaulding Fuller works on sculpting the new Predator head, providing further evidence that all artists subconsciously include a self-portrait in their work. The model-kit toy on his sculpting stand proved to be useful reference on more than one occasion when trying to identify the "Predator design aesthetic."

06 An entire team of talented sculptors, including Mike O'Brien, forged the Predator armor out of water-based clay.

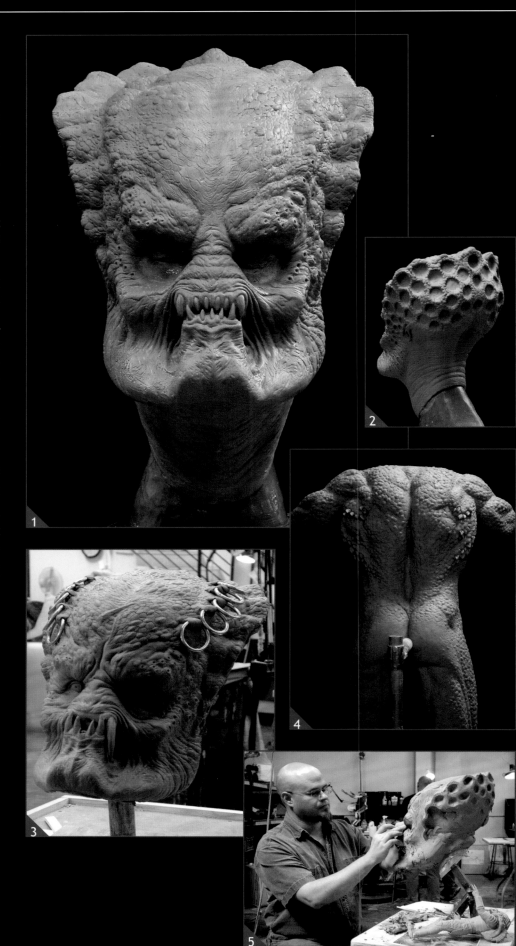

6

51

1

01 ADI founders Alec Gillis and Tom Woodruff, Jr. make frequent tours of the shop to check on progress, answer questions, and address any potential problems or concerns. Here they discuss a sculpture of a Predator backpack with sculptor Bruce Spaulding Fuller.

02 Sculpting Supervisor Andy Schoneberg listens as Alec Gillis gives his thoughts on the progress of the Predator's body armor.

03 The completed sculpture for the Predator net gun. The wooden supports are the beginning of the molding process.

04 A close-up of some of the tribal carvings on the mandible tusks of the Predator Elders.

2

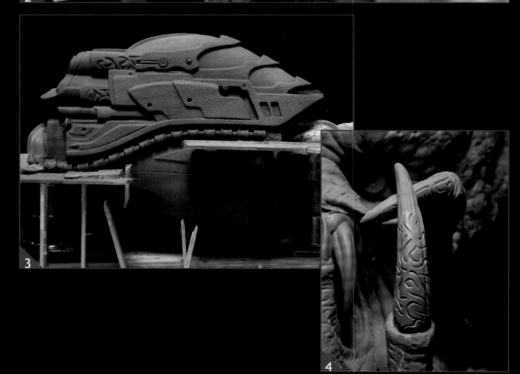

3

4

05 The finished sculpture of Scar's wrist blade housing.

06 and 07 Two examples of collaboration between the sculpting and model-making departments. The organic knife handle and spear accents were sculpted out of clay, while the blades, which needed extremely clean and sharp edges, were fashioned out of plastic compounds.

08 Size 20? Tom Woodruff, Jr. examines a sculpture of the Predator foot.

01 The finished sculpture of a Predator Elder's helmet.

02 Multiple views of the helmet of the Predator that came to be known as "Chopper" by the crew in Prague.

03 A close-up view of the Elder helmet in photograph 01 on page 54. Some of the more intricately detailed parts came from toy model kits.

04 This Elder helmet was intentionally designed to echo the helmet in the original *Predator*.

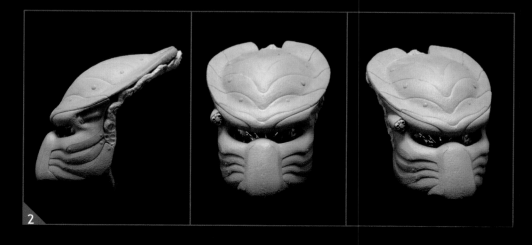

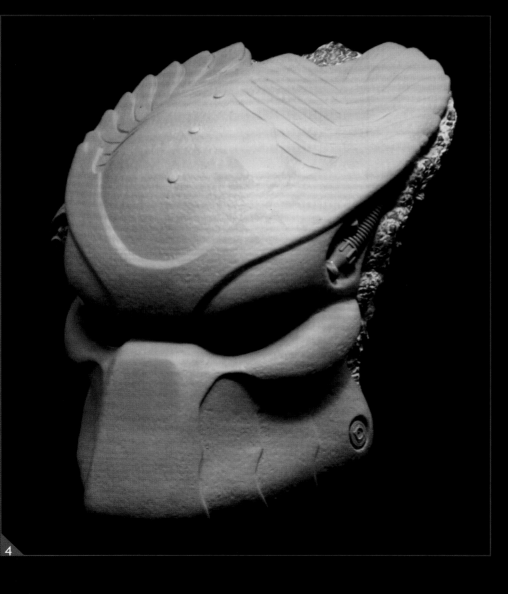

3

4

BRUCE SPAULDING FULLER
Sculptor

Famous Monsters of Filmland Magazine exposed Bruce to the creations of make-up legends like Lon Chaney and Jack Pierce—the same monsters he'd watch on TV. Bruce realized you didn't need cadavers to make monsters, instead raiding his mom's make-up drawer for supplies. His passion for monsters fueled his persistence to develop his talent as a sculptor, but the Art Students League of N.Y. and subsequent careers in advertising and freelance illustration left him restless. Instead, a chance meeting with Ed French in N.Y. led him into the world of professional make-up effects as he soon found himself working in L.A. A fan of the original *Predator*, Bruce was the only artist who worked on *Predator 2* and continued the legacy on *AVP*.

JEFF BUCCACIO
Sculptor

Originally from Boston, Jeff was another ADI "discovery." Starting on *Alien Resurrection*, he's racked up credits like *Starship Troopers*, and *Santa Clause 2*. Jeff is a trained sculptor and his knowledge of anatomy has made him a sought after artist. *Alien, Aliens,* and *Predator* were three of his favorite movies, but he confesses that he was scared wiggly by *Pumpkinhead* (Tom sometimes threatens to don that suit again for motivational purposes). Jeff enjoyed sculpting the third-scale Predator, giving him a chance to flex his sculptural muscles while sculpting the Predator's flexed muscles. Though he spent much of his youth singing in his parents' band, these days the only serenading Jeff does is to his wife, Nina Marie.

01 Using the few available reference photos and dark, blurry, screen captures from *Predator*, the original shoulder cannon was painstakingly recreated to be as authentic as possible.

02 The Predator's sternum plate was sculpted on a cast of his chest to ensure a snug fit.

03 Likewise, the shin guards were sculpted on castings of the feet. These would ultimately be produced as a single piece of foam latex. The Predator performers could slip on these "booties" which then would be glued down to the legs of the body suits and covered with armor to hide any seams.

04 The finished Predator backpack unit. Like some of the helmets, interesting-looking bits from model kits were used to quickly add some visual detail. Also, the repeating shell-like forms on the backside were mimicked on the net gun to help give the entire armor a cohesive aesthetic.

Opposite: Steve Koch sculpts from his heart as he works on the Predator's sole.

Now We Just Have to Build It

After it's completed, something happens to a sculpture, which usually gets glossed over in the "making of" books. The sentence often reads something like this: "Once finished, the sculpture is molded and skins are produced so that geniuses called *airbrush artists* can work their magic!" Well, the folks who make those molds and produce those skins are pretty smart too. Mold making is a technical skill that, although it has been around since the Bronze Age, has reached its zenith right here and now. The wide array of materials available to the mold-maker is overwhelming. Plasters, polyesters, urethanes, silicones (do you prefer tin or platinum?), epoxies, vinyls, acrylics are all choices, and each category has many types within it. The mold-maker must know everything about these products as each one is used in a specific situation. For instance, certain silicones won't set up against certain clays. Imagine arriving at the studio in the morning and discovering that the sculpture that was labored over for weeks is now submerged in a gooey, taffy-like mess, because you picked the wrong silicone. The boss is screaming and the schedule is completely blown. This is the kind of pressure that a mold-maker lives with. But, if you know your stuff, mold making can be a fun mental challenge. You see, molds are actually designed. Their construction doesn't just happen. Somebody (or a team of somebodies) stares at a sculpture for hours and figures out where the dividing line must go

to avoid undercuts, what type of skin material will be injected into the mold, and how it can be made as user-friendly as possible. Skin thickness must be decided, in tandem with the mechanical designers, and internal forms, or cores, are then produced as well. Mold-makers are also responsible for making the body shells that are attached to the articulated structures the mechanical designers build. These shells are critical, as any malformation will affect the shape of the skin lying on top. A shell that is too heavy can slow down or otherwise hinder the performance of the Animatronic puppet.

Mold-makers are also often responsible for the castings that come out of the molds. The fiberglass heads of the Aliens and the armor masks of the Predators needed to be as lightweight as possible, since performers wear them. The mandate at ADI was that everything that comes out of a mold must be lightweight and strong, and there's an art to that.

ADI's mold shop produced hundreds of molds for *AVP* from many different materials. Enormous fiberglass molds of the queen, intricate epoxy molds of the Predator's mandibles, and silicone molds of Predator weapons and armor were created with great care and precision. But for all this effort, the mold-maker's work is not directly seen in the final film. This is entirely appropriate, because molds are just plain ugly. But when the mold-maker does the job right, the integrity of the sculpture is kept intact, and the finished work is that much more effective.

Opposite: The unfinished head of an Alien Warrior lies in wait of a skilled pair of hands to ready it for the silver screen.

Above: Slimy yet satisfying? Neil Winn pours silicone rubber to create a mold of Predator thigh armor.

The other half of this equation is the production of the skins and their preparation for painting. Like mold-making, there is a myriad of choices of skin materials to be considered. Foam latex, the industry workhorse, has beautiful compression and stretch, but is opaque. Silicone is translucent, but is very heavy and weak. Urethanes can be translucent, but are ultra-violet sensitive and toxic. Even the method of getting the material into the mold must be examined. Will the foam latex be injected or brushed in? Can the silicone be poured into the mold, or does it require a pressure pot because the voids are too thin for gravity to ensure a proper fill? Sometimes "bleeder holes" are drilled into the crannies of a mold to allow trapped air to escape and the rubber to fill the void. While this prevents large air bubbles in the skin, it also leaves stems of material that must be patched. The more patching that is done, the further the skin gets from the original sculpted texture and form. Not ideal, but sometimes necessary.

Above: Tony Matijevich dresses an Animatronic face-hugger puppet by sliding hollow foam latex appendages over its mechanized skeleton.

Below: Worker bees buzz about the hive. During the course of *AVP*'s frenzied period of creation, ADI enlisted the talents of over 100 artists and technicians.

Below, top to bottom: Dustin Van Housen thinks it's a good thing that the Alien head he is working on is made out of fiberglass and not Kryptonite.

Seaming a palm as large as her head, Christina Prestia literally lends a hand to the monumental effort of creating the creatures of *AVP*.

Nevada Smith drills holes into an Alien skull in preparation for attaching its plastic dome.

Above: Dwarfed by the imposing mass of a fiberglass mold of the Alien Queen head carapace, Mike Manzel goes about his mold shop duties.

In the case of *AVP*, we opted to use foam latex for most of the skins. The script called for physical action beyond what had been previously attempted in a Predator or Alien film. Durability of the suits was a huge issue. We couldn't afford to discard a suit after only one or two days of use. The other issue was of performer comfort (did we say "comfort"?). The heavier the suit, the quicker performance disappears and becomes an endurance test. Because Tom plays the Alien, he is intimately familiar with those problems, and is personally involved in designing solutions to them. Foam latex was really the best choice of material for the body suits of both Alien and Predator.

Like the mold-makers, the work of artists who create, patch and seam skins is invisible in the final film. After all, invisibility is what makes the Predators and Aliens so deadly, isn't it? (Wow. What a lousy closing sentence.)

01 While most of the Predator shuriken, or throwing discs, were made of lightweight resin, specific scenes called for some to be of a more durable nature. For reinforcement, steel plates were acid-cut to the proper shape and inserted into the mold before the resin was cast. Mold Shop Supervisor Jim Leonard finesses one of the steel inserts on a grinding wheel.

02 Brandon Whynaucht prepares a queen hand to be molded. Molds from previous installments of the Alien film franchise were used for the full-size queen arms, forearms, legs, tail, and face. Her hands, torso, and head carapace were all freshly sculpted for *AVP*.

03 In the ADI Mold Shop, crew members lay small sheets of fiberglass saturated with a polyester resin to create a mold of the full-size queen head.

04 Davis Fandiño builds a clay wall to mold one of the queen's back spines.

05 Steve Munson assembles a urethane quarter-scale queen for an early production meeting with the director and producers of *AVP*.

06 Johnnie Saiko Espiritu watches as Bryan Blair works on a mold of an Alien Warrior hand.

07 Despite appearances, Pete Farrell and Neil Winn are not shrink-wrapping Predator actor Ian Whyte for sale in the freezer section. They are making a "snap mold" of his torso to provide an accurate template on which to sculpt his body armor.

08 Rob Freitas cleans a silicone casting of a Predator head.

1

2

3

4

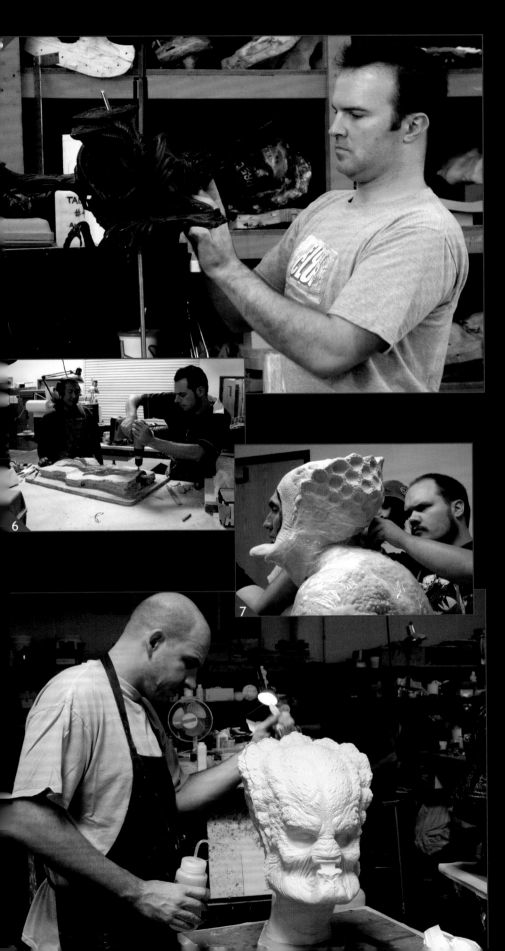

GARTH WINKLESS
Assistant Shop Supervisor

Garth grew up in a show business fam
that included his grandfather, dad, uncl
(Bingo, Drooper, and Fleegle of T
Banana Splits), and siblings working
writers, actors, directors, costumers,
special effects technicians and puppetee
in film and television. A high-falutin' B.S.
Biology encouraged Garth toward acade
ic pursuits like producing detailed, hig
accurate models of dinosaurs before t
Winkless showbiz blood kicked in and
moved from Albuquerque to L.A. Althou
he's worked for several major effects hou
es, Garth has spent most of his time with
on Spider-Man 1 & 2, Starship Troope
Alien Resurrection, and many others.
skills, resourcefulness, and dedicati
make him as valuable on set as in the sh

TIM LEACH
Finishing Supervisor

A native of Long Beach, California, T
was inspired specifically "by some mo
with cool effects." While at Cal State Lo
Beach he studied make-up and la
became a student of Dick Smith's ma
up course. He brings 20 years of exp
ence to AVP, having spent about 10
them at ADI. His credits include Juma
Starship Troopers, Alien Resurrecti
Bubble Boy, and Spider-Man. Tim a
was an important member of the film
crew in Prague, dealing with unexpec
catastrophes like when the queen's
ton-powered tongue fired prematur
causing severe tooth damage. Tim
now add Alien dentistry to his list of qu
fications. Long Beach is still home to T
Dana, and their sons, Taylor and Dary

01 Chris Grossnickle, Rob Freitas, Mike Manzel, and Pete Farrell paint the foam sculpture of the queen body to seal it before it is molded.

02 Nevada Smith attaches a transparent dome to the head of a warrior.

03 Tony McCray pours urethane foam into cylindrical molds to produce lightweight Predator dreadlocks of varying sizes.

04 Foam Supervisor Roland Blancaflor and Rob Freitas confer over the body mold of the Alien Queen. (Contrary to popular belief, shaving your head is not required to work in the special effects industry.)

05 Mike Arbios inspects a resin casting of a Predator shuriken fresh from the mold. Luckily for his co-workers he decided not to "see how she flies!"

06 ADI was enlisted to take a life cast of actor Lance Henriksen (Weyland) which would later be turned over to Animated Extras, the company that handled *AVP*'s human Make-up Effects, to create a replica head. Andy Schoneberg starts the process by applying a bald cap.

07 After covering Henriksen in quick-curing alginate, Mold Shop Supervisor Jim Leonard, Mike Manzel, and Andy Schoneberg start applying a layer of plaster bandages. When done properly, the whole process should take only about two hours including prep and clean-up (the subject should only be under the alginate and plaster for about twenty minutes) and cause relatively little discomfort.

ARTIST PROFILE

JIM LEONARD
Mold Shop Supervisor

As a child, images of monsters on the drive-in theater screen in Indiana weren't enough. They became real in Jim's dreams. An accidental meeting with Don Post, Jr. had Don telling Jim he would never achieve his dream in Indiana. Jim trekked to L.A. in 1979 where he worked for the veteran mask-maker for awhile before hooking up with the master, Rick Baker. Rising to become the premiere mold-maker, Jim also developed his own sculpting talents in personal projects. It was a rare and unexpected bonus to have him on the *AVP* team. His skill and positive attitude extend to the kids of today, "Stay focused and reach for the best you have in you. Anything in life that you want...go for it!"

ROLAND BLANCAFLOR
Foam Shop Supervisor

Although *AVP* was Roland's first job at ADI, he is no stranger to Make-up and Animatronics. He's spent 17 years in the industry, and is renowned as a foam latex specialist who brings innovation to every project. With the help of his talented foam crew, he produced high quality foam latex suits and Animatronic skins with a low reject rate. Considering that *AVP* is, in Roland's words, "the largest creature suit film of all time," that's no small accomplishment. Roland's influences in the field were Lon Chaney, Dick Smith, Rick Baker and his own father. Foam running is a nebulous discipline: part chemistry, part cooking. Roland brings a refreshingly practical approach to the work. You'll see more of Roland's work in future ADI projects!

5

6

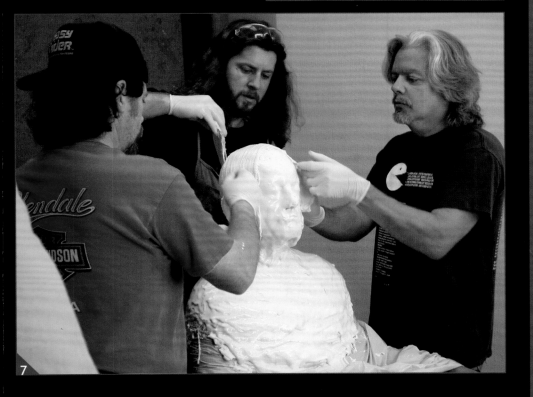

7

01 Mike Manzel, Davis Fandiño, and Steve Munson prep a silicone body mold of Predator actor Ian Whyte.

02 The Predator body sculpture in the process of being molded. The bright yellow color comes from a sealing coat of shellac and the thin metal shims mark the split line of the two halves of the mold.

03 Don't they know it's after Labor Day? ADI's white-garbed foam crew brushes a skin layer of foam latex into first one half, then the other half, of an Alien Warrior body mold. Next, the two halves will be sealed around a spandex bodysuit held in place by an inner "core." After more foam has been injected to fill the gap between the skin layer and the spandex, the entire mold will be placed inside a walk-in oven for several hours to cure.

04 If you have an aversion to syringes, you may want to avoid getting into the foam business. Foam Supervisor Roland Blancaflor uses an exceptionally large one to inject foam into the wrist of the Predator body mold.

05 Bill Fesh contemplates the size of the omelet he could make with one of ADI's industrial-sized foam mixers.

06 Cory Czekaj and Roland Blancaflor brush foam rubber into a mold of an Alien tail.

07 In a flurry of activity Matt Mastrella and John Calpin emerge from the ADI foam room armed with syringes full of foam destined to become one of the many Alien skins created for *AVP*. Successful foam-running is a delicate combination of chemistry, experience, and hustle. Once a batch of foam is prepared, it is essential to get it into the mold quickly before the natural curing process causes it to "gel" (where it is no longer fluid enough to seep into all the minute details of the mold).

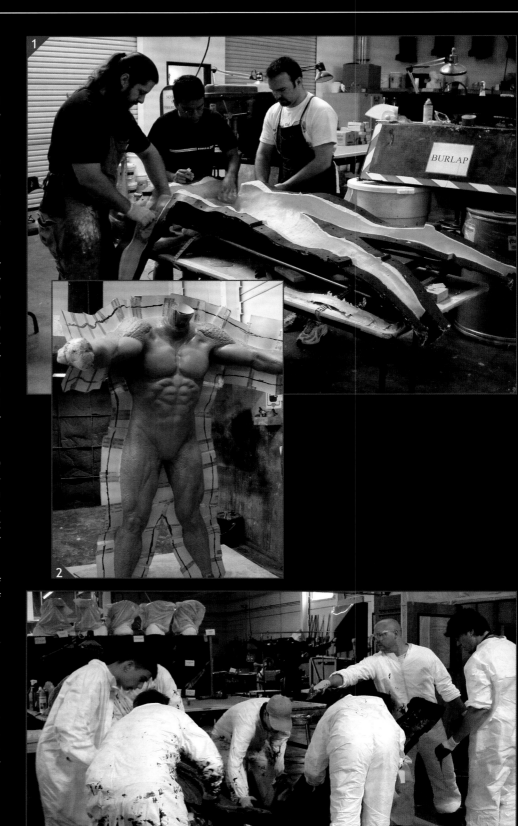

TAMARA CARLSON-WOODARD
Fabrication Department Head

Santa Clause 2 was TaMara's first job at ADI, but *AVP* was her biggest challenge. "The amount of work on *AVP* was incredible!" she says. "Each armored Predator had over 40 individual parts. Making sure each piece of every suit was interchangeable was an accomplishment the whole Fabrication Department should be proud of!" TaMara's love of her craft began with her love of the work of Jim Henson and the Muppets, specifically *Labyrinth* and *The Dark Crystal*. After graduating from make-up school, she discovered the world of effects in 1994. She's married to Scott, and they have two cats and a dog rescued from a Romanian film set. Long hours drive her to do inexplicable things like put up backwards clocks. She calls her multi-colored hair "a cry for help."

TONY MATIJEVICH
Finishing Department

There's a dark and scary place inside Tony's head. A black landscape etched in the grey matter through an obsessive fixation with Biblical art and avant-garde photography. Mix that with a love of Disneyland and Winnie the Pooh, and you've got the perfect ADI employee! Tony's been with us since '94 and has piled up 26 movie credits. He's a well-rounded artist, but his sure hand and focus on detail has planted him firmly in the Finishing Department. He's the guy who usually applies the skins to our most sophisticated Animatronics, making sure they retain their sculptural shape, and don't restrict the mechanisms. Watch for his work in an unusual place: his company, Morevil Art, provided many of the skulls adorning the Predator's costume!

01 Bryan Blair reinforces a queen head carapace with fiberglass.

02 At one point in the film, the Alien Queen is exposed to the blast from a Predator bomb, resulting in a cracked and disfigured carapace. An undamaged shell of the head was back-filled with polyfoam and then cracks and holes were carved through the fiberglass surface. After this has been done, Mike Manzel sprays it with a primer coat with help from Andy Schoneberg.

03 Since the damaged queen would be realized at multiple scales, the look was first designed at quarter-scale, photographed, and enlarged to full-scale on the computer. Chris Ayers tiles prints together to help the sculptors accurately transfer the crack patterns to the larger head.

04 With the detailing stage complete, Mike Manzel wheels the damaged queen head to the Paint Department.

05 Ginger Anglin seams a Predator head after the foam latex has been baked and removed from the mold.

06 Kathy Sully helps prepare a Predator stunt dummy which was used for shots of dead Predators.

07 Even extra-terrestrial species need dental maintenance once in awhile. Rob Freitas adjusts the dummy's armature before the mandibles are added.

08 The nearly finished dummy awaits a trip to the paint department.

1

2

3

4

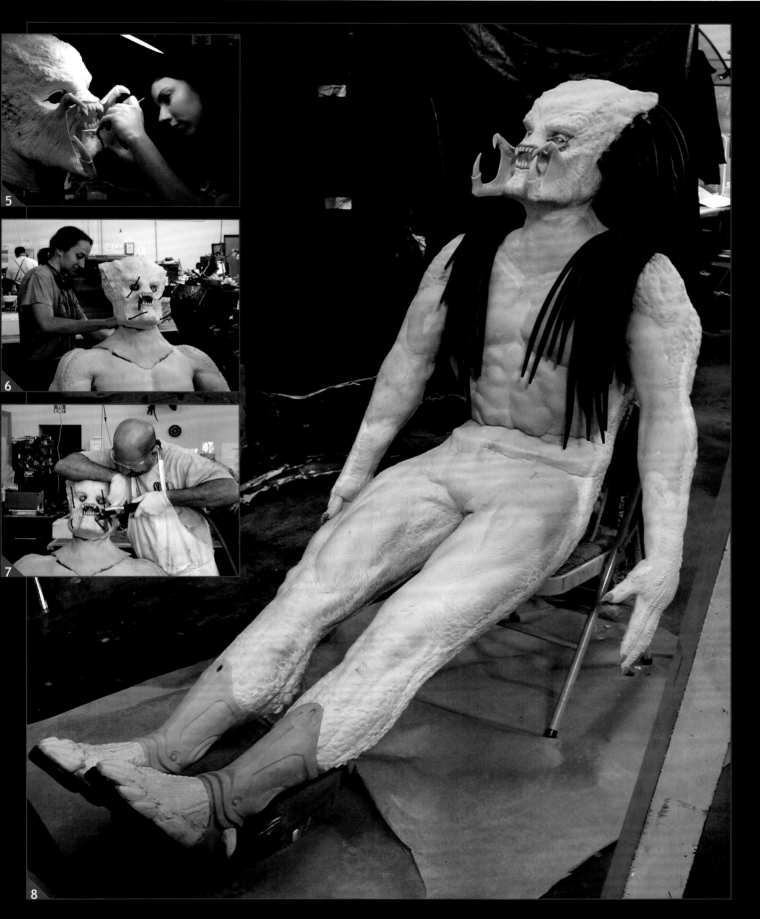

01 While Mike Manzel places shims along the top of the queen's egg sac, Rob Freitas nonchalantly tackles the less-accessible regions.

02 Steve Kuzela seams the neck of an Alien Warrior.

03 An estimated 1,000 Predator dreadlocks were made for *AVP*.

04 Christina Prestia is on sponge duty as she lays down small amounts of latex to patch a Predator skin while Brian Clawson follows in her steps with a hairdryer to cure the freshly laid patches.

05 What might appear as an interstellar bear hug is actually Brian Clawson patching a Predator suit.

06 Sean Kennedy tunes out any distractions and focuses on tidying up an Alien foot.

07 Against the backdrop of a Predator armory, Jon Fedele seams a chestburster.

08 Take your pick: Patricia Urias seams the tail of either a facehugger or a chestburster. A single, interchangeable sculpture was used for the posteriors of both stages of the Alien life cycle.

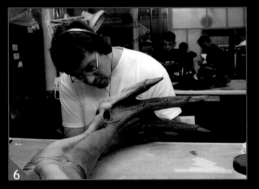

ARTIST PROFILE

KAREN KEENER-MANZEL
Finishing Department

What if your mom was an animator on *Sleeping Beauty* and *101 Dalmations*, and as a kid you were enthralled by *An American Werewolf in London*? Naturally you'd become...*a lawyer*? Karen almost did until she put her soul on trial and the verdict came back GUILTY (of being an effects fan). She was sentenced to life in the business, and so far has served 15 years, much of it at ADI. Some of her credits include *Mortal Kombat*, *Jumanji*, *Starship Troopers*, and *Alien Resurrection*. Karen works with rubber, fur, feathers and now her husband Mike, whom she met while working on the remake of *Planet of the Apes*. They're both in it for life and consider themselves "soul mates" (or is it cell mates?).

THASJA HOFFMANN
Purchaser

At the Art Institute of Chicago, Thasja's artistic inspiration by masters such as Matisse was supplemented by the cinematic transformations of *The Nutty Professor* and the love of the idea of altering living forms. Arriving in Los Angeles in 2000, Thasja worked hard as a make-up artist on many independent films for over a year. Through a friend she met Tom Woodruff, Jr. and joined ADI's art department on *Spider-Man*, *Santa Clause 2*, and of course, *AVP*. We are grateful for her flexibility to switch gears and apply her hard-working nature, professionalism, and enthusiasm to the office rather than the art department for a change (don't worry, she's already back in the art department, refurbishing the Alien Queen to be returned to Bob Burns)!

01 TaMara Carlson-Woodard affixes closures to an Alien suit while Leticia Sandoval works on a shiny Predator backpack that has yet to be aged and dirtied by the Paint Department.

02 John Calpin comes face-to-chin with a foam latex skin of the queen.

03 Ivonne Escoto cleans a casting of a third-scale Predator sculpture.

04 David Brooke administers a steady hand to a warrior's head. The vacuum-formed plastic dome and foam facial skin, including lips and jaw tendons, will soon be added.

05 Christine Papalexis at work in the Fabrication Department. On this show, Fabrication was responsible for taking all the individual Alien and Predator skin and armor pieces and fashioning them into durable and comfortable (at least as comfortable as possible) finished suits.

06 Naomi Gathmann works on a section of Predator body netting. The thickness, weave pattern, color, and material of the netting all had to be discussed, designed, and approved.

07 Brieana Bellis attaches foam dreadlocks to a Predator mask.

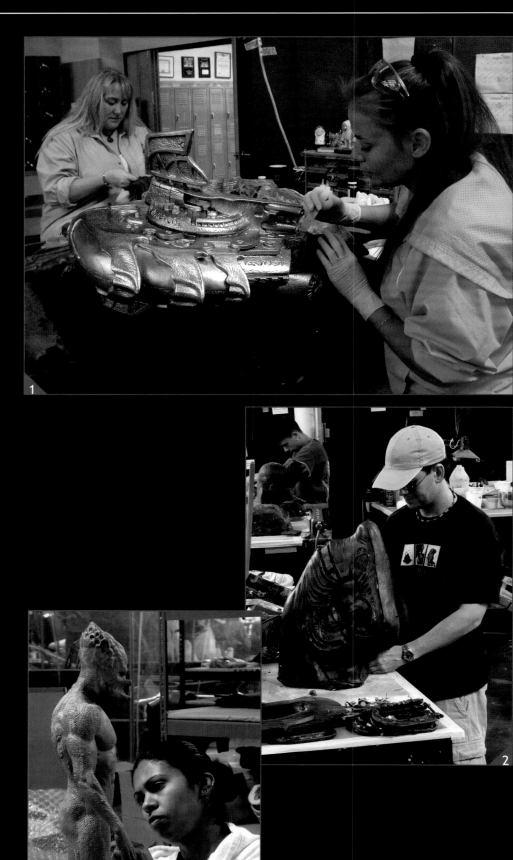

ARTIST PROFILE

TAMMY MINGUS
Office Manager

Tammy hails from the wilds of Wisconsin, where it hails wildly. Prior to her emigration to L.A., her job highlights included four years at a cheese factory, where she supervised the processing and packaging of all types of cheeses (Fridays was "curd day"). Bolstered by her unfettered success at one cheese factory, she set her sights on another, and moved to Hollywood. After one week in L.A., she landed a job at ADI and has been here since. L.A.'s beautiful weather suits the athletic Tammy, who is an avid Roller Hockey player. She hasn't adopted the local diet, however, preferring coco powder paste, fried foods and avoiding fruits and vegetables. Tammy is in charge of the people behind the behind-the-scenes people who keep ADI running smooth as Velveeta.

NICOLE MICHAUD
Production Coordinator

Nicki has a B.A. in fine art from Hartwick College in N.Y., and 20 years experience as a watercolorist and architectural renderer. So how'd she end up with an office job? Back on *Santa Clause 2,* when we needed extra office help, her fiancé, Andy Schoneberg recommended her. Since then she's worked at ADI on *Looney Tunes: Back in Action, Spider-Man 2, Scary Movie III,* and of course, *AVP.* Building in L.A. and shooting in Prague presented enormous shipping challenges, which she tackled with her usual thoroughness. Nicki has also been inspired to expand her creative skill package by learning sculpture and wig making. Soon you may see her name in the credits of a movie as one of the artists!

01 With Ginger Anglin's help, Her Majesty the Queen begins to take shape and comes ever nearer to wreaking havoc on the big screen.

02 If they were palm readers, they would have their work cut out for them. Dawn Dininger and TaMara Carlson-Woodard work on a pair of Queen hands.

Opposite: Matt Killen installs a set of vicious-looking clear urethane teeth into the queen's mouth. Hopefully she's not hungry.

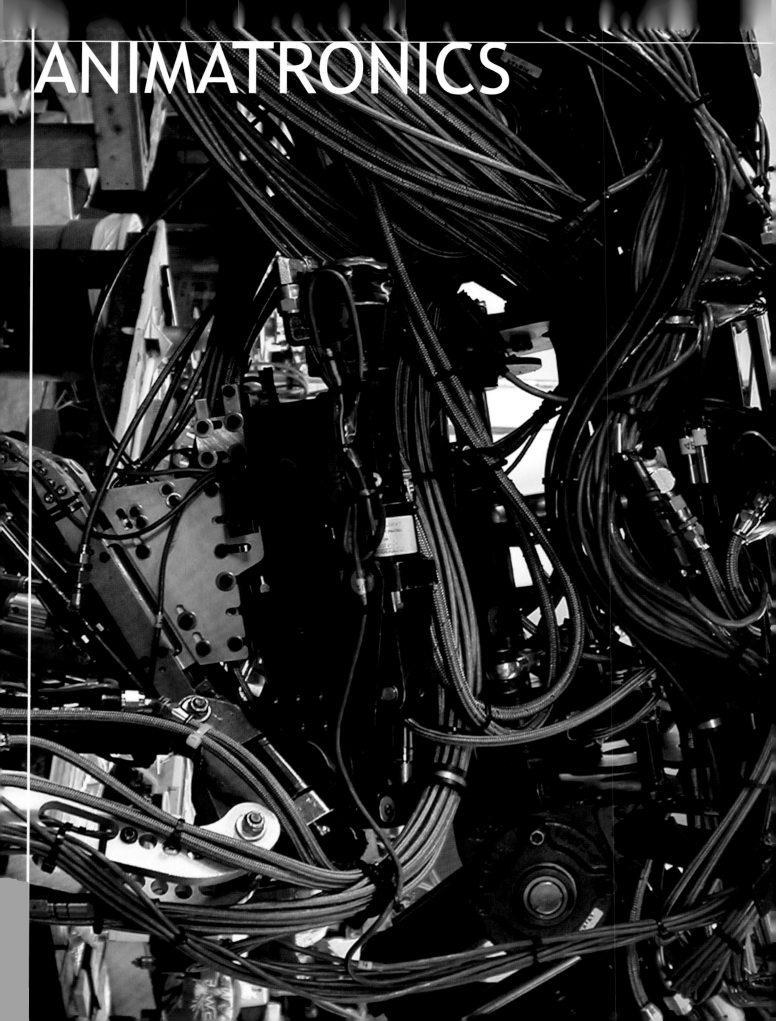

ANIMATRONICS

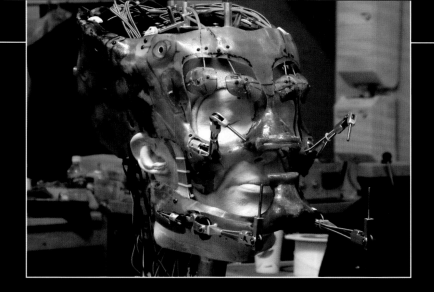

Nuts, Bolts, & Thermal Evaculometers

P art of the goal of this book is to sing the praises of the unsung heroes of visual effects. Much is made of the efforts of those involved in creating what you see on screen, but what about what's *inside* what you see? That is the work of the many mechanical designers, machinists, computer experts, and electrical designers that create the brains, the heart, and the muscle of an Animatronic creature.

For *AVP*, ADI's workspace was split down the middle, with about half the space going to art and half to mechanical (the "split" is imaginary, since the studio space is actually one large open room—we prefer it that way because it encourages communication between departments, and the crew is free to circulate and look at the inspiring work of others). There are no closed doors to create divisions, except bathroom doors—that's where you want divisions (and air fresheners).

As with other departments, we were fortunate to have key people we'd worked with previously, so that sped up communication. In addition, since we've built characters with each other before, there's a history to draw upon. We can say, "Remember that gimble joint on *Starship* with the external thingy, let's do that but put the thingy *inside* this time", and they'll know what we mean. Shorthand communication was important because we had to hit the ground running if we were going to meet our aggressive deadlines. We had a huge amount of work to do in four and a half months, and the mechanical department got even less time

because much of their work couldn't begin until sculptures and molds were completed. Our team consisted of twenty-five crew members responsible for everything ranging from direct cable-controlled puppets to complex servo/hydraulic Animatronics.

Cable actuated mechanisms are the "old standby" of the creature business. The technique has been around for a long time (Willis O'Brien built a brontosaurus head and neck this way in the original *King Kong*), but has been refined over the years. The idea is that, like a bicycle brake, you squeeze a trigger (or pull a lever, or turn a pulley), which pulls a cable, and something moves at the other end. It's a good, powerful way of articulating something, as long as you can deal with a bundle of cables exiting the puppet. The Alien eggs were built this way, along with a four-foot length of Alien tail.

The most sophisticated cable puppet built for the project was the third-scale Queen Alien puppet. This puppet was used mostly in shots of the captive Queen in her chamber, rising out of the deep-freeze, and later being forced to lay eggs, subsequently going berserk and breaking free of her restraints.

Radio controlled (R.C.) electric servo motors are another way to articulate puppets. This is where the term "Animatronics" comes from. Disney's Imagineering coined the phrase back when they were developing technology for the theme parks. It refers to animation through electronics, and has since become a catchall phrase for any sophisticated film puppet work.

Above: One of the hero Animatronic Predator heads before its foam latex skin has been applied.
Opposite: To the untrained eye, this may appear to be an unruly mass of wires, cables and bits of

metal abstraction. To an ADI mechanic, however, how could it be anything other than the torso of a hydraulic Alien Queen?

Above: The ADI mechanical staff gathers to test the motion capabilities of the queen one last time before she is crated up and shipped to Prague.

Opposite: Seth Hays takes our pet facehugger for a walk in the ADI display room to test its mechanics.

To our knowledge, the phrase has not been copyrighted, but if there are any Disney lawyers reading this now, please serve all papers directly to Stan Winston.

Anyway, R.C. is great for self-contained mechanisms, and lends itself to wonderfully subtle facial articulation. The motors themselves are very responsive, and the puppeteering process is more ergonomic than with cable mechanisms. Since the motors do the work, the puppeteer uses fingertip control joysticks (or other input devices) that prioritize performance over brute strength. Also, certain functions can be "mixed" electronically so that multiple servos move together automatically, giving a more synchronized performance. The hero Alien heads and Predator heads were articulated this way. Subtlety of facial expression was especially critical to the Predator, as he was to be a more sympathetic character this time around. Recent advances in smaller, more powerful motors helped us give him a greater range of movement than was previously possible.

Another project that benefited by the use of R.C. was the hero facehugger. We knew that the facehugger action as described in Paul's script would require lots of floppy stunt facehuggers and hand puppeted facehuggers. We also knew that we wanted to improve on the style of mechanical puppet seen thus far. For our hero facehugger, we built a combination cable and R.C. mechanism. The body of the facehugger was too small to effectively fit motors in, so we built an external "motor pack" that actuated the cables running to the mechanism inside the puppet's body. This

gave the puppeteers the delicate, fluid control that elevated *AVP*'s facehugger to a new level of creepiness.

A long-term dream of ours has been to create an Alien Warrior that was completely mechanical. On *AVP*, we finally had that opportunity. The goal for this particular character was to build in movements impossible to achieve with a performer in a suit. The torso had increased ranges of movement, as did the neck, which was capable of turning the head 180 degrees around to look directly behind it. The neck also had a cobra-like striking ability, and the head carried a pneumatic tongue. This sophisticated puppet was performed with the help of a computer motion control system, which not only aided in performance, but was a safety must for operating in close quarter combat with a performer in a Predator suit.

The most formidable creature in the film was also the most formidable one to design and build. *AVP*'s updated Alien Queen had to be faster, leaner and meaner than her predecessor, and she had to be built quickly and reliably. In our business everything we create is essentially a prototype, without benefit of extensive testing followed by rebuilding. It is ADI's history of successful Animatronic characters that we draw from when creating the next one. The queen is a direct descendent of Comet the reindeer from *Santa Clause 2*, which was preceded by *Alien Resurrection*'s Newborn, which followed characters from *Starship Troopers, My Favorite Martian, Jumanji*, etc. Everything we've learned goes into the next one, and we are always seeking improvement in all areas. The tricky part is balancing the desire to innovate with the inherent risks of experimentation.

At the end of the day, something dynamic yet reliable had better show up on set, and *AVP*'s Queen was both. With forty-seven points of hydraulic movement, she may well have more movement than any other Animatronic in history (don't you get sick of claims like that?). Hydraulics was the only way to get the kind of power and speed needed for a fifteen-foot tall rampaging Alien.

Hydraulics work like this: A huge pump moves oil through a hose and into a cylinder. As the cylinder fills with oil it pushes out a rod. That powerful piston action is transferred into any kind of motion desired. It's as simple as that (OK, it's much more technical, but that's the basic idea). It really gets complicated when you calculate mass and inertia and the creature's own body weight and how many pounds per square inch of oil are needed to move it at what speed, and on and on. All that gets boring real quick, which is why we hire smart people who actually enjoy that kind of brain work.

We approach mechanical design from the outside in. Our emphasis is always on the performance and practicality of a given character. We enjoy working with mechanical designers who don't look at their creations as robots, but as characters. On *AVP*, we were fortunate to have exactly that.

Earlier we said that the mechanical department creates the brains, heart and muscle of an Animatronic character. If the hydraulics is the "muscle," and the pump is the "heart," what then, is the "brain?" The brain is the motion control computer. In the case of the queen, there are actually two brains. One computer is external to the puppet, and it interfaces the signals sent from the puppeteering controls to the other onboard computer. The onboard computer interprets the data sent from the puppeteering controls and relays that info to the servo valves, which regulate the flow of oil to the cylinders.

The motion control system we used on *AVP* is the latest in an evolution that goes back to 1995's *Starship Troopers*. At that time we were developing a proprietary motion control system that put an emphasis on performance and editing, but included features like collision avoidance, and movement smoothing compliance. Fast forward to 2004, and our former motion control expert has formed his own company, Concept Overdrive, and has created the Overdrive Control System. This is the most puppeteer-friendly system we've worked with, and it allows a great deal of flexibility in pre-recording and playback of performances. It also has redundant failsafe systems that give the puppeteers confidence in operating this powerful creature in close proximity to actors.

For all the technical complexities presented by *AVP*, there were no significant mechanical failures while filming on set. More importantly, the creatures

performed convincingly and organically. One way to measure the effectiveness of the creatures in a film is by looking in the eyes of the actors who share the scene with them. Even though it is a creation of steel and rubber, when an actor stares into the wet maw of the Queen Alien, it doesn't take much technique or method to pull up an emotion. It's already there...because it's real.

ARTIST PROFILE

DAVE PENIKAS
Mechanical Supervisor

With an interest so diverse as to include R.C. model flying, electronics, and 8mm filmmaking, a youthful Dave Penikas spent many of his early, formative years blowing things up* for home movies. Maybe this accounts for his fascination with what the *insides* of things look like. Although certainly finding inspiration in the work of Ray Harryhausen, Dave was much more interested in building a stop-motion armature than trying to sculpt a finished creature. *Star Wars* and the work of John Dykstra were also heavily influential as the world of model-making and miniatures caught his attention.

Throughout high school, Dave would find odd jobs at effects houses in the L.A. area. He found a job to do some wiring on a talking Teddy Bear character for a TV show, but his familiarity with servo motors from years of flying model planes had him working on full Animatronic character heads almost immediately. From there Dave moved onward and upward, becoming even more fascinated with Animatronics and mechanical design, as he first set foot in the Hell-spawned halls of ADI.

Modest to a fault, Dave will not tell you that he has become a staple for the last ten years here (in fact, Dave's resume reads almost the same as ADI's). As Mechanical Supervisor, he has become the best Animatronic guy around and is responsible for bringing to life some of our most notable creatures over the years.

The same hands that can tear out an Oleander tree at home on the weekend can create the most subtle and successful Animatronic heads in the industry on a Monday. When he's not achieving some incredible deadline at work, flying model helicopters, renovating his home, learning the world of computer animation, building a tree fort for his kids, or camping, Dave enjoys spending time with his wife Theresa and his kids, Andrew and Alexis.

*Disclaimer: ADI does not advocate the leisurely use of explosive devices—Detonate Responsibly.

01 Nevada Smith mixes up a small batch of epoxy while working on one of several "Grid" effects heads. These heads, rigged with extra "plumbing" for blood and smoke, would be used for close-up insert shots of "Grid" caught in a Predator's net.

02 Seth Hays rigs a wire-work harness for Tom Woodruff's Alien suit.

03 An Alien egg prior to being sheathed in a silicone skin (and lots of slime.) ADI was able to refurbish the inner mechanics of the eggs from previous Alien films for *AVP.*

04 A warrior head in the process of being fabricated. A foam skin will be glued to the metal cables running across the lip area. These cables can be radio-controlled to retract and lift, creating the Alien's signature snarl.

05 As part of its R&D phase, Tom Woodruff, Jr. designed a bungee harness that would allow increased opportunities for creating Alien-like movements practically instead of digitally. The body harness saw extensive action because it was less bulky than traditional harnesses. Here, Woodruff test-crawls the harness for the first time.

06 Seth Hays fastens an unfinished Alien headpiece to Tom Woodruff.

07 Steve Koch shoots test footage of a mocked-up set where the shop floor represents a wall (note the clock) and the black plastic sheeting represents the ceiling. The down-angle on Seth Hays (lying prone on a bench) creates the illusion of a victim leaning against the "wall." Tom Woodruff, Jr. assumes his role as an Alien stalking its prey from above.

STEVE ROSENBLUTH
Mechanical Designer

Steve got into special effects, not because of science fiction, but because he loved inventing and building things. At fourteen, he was building props for his friends' Super-8 films. Having studied Psychology, Literature, and Sculpture in school, he credits that broad Liberal Arts background for giving him the ability to be creative in a high-tech realm. Starting as a model-maker and painter, Steve taught himself the technology and is now *the* control systems expert to turn to for Animatronic characters. He designed the Overdrive control system which actuated the hydraulic warrior and Alien Queen, "The most complex hydraulic we've ever controlled." Steve lives in Burbank with his wife, Helene and their low-tech cat, Mao.

JEFF EDWARDS
Mechanical Designer

In 1988, shortly after attending the Art Institute of Seattle, Jeff found himself working at a fledgling effects company called ADI. The film was *Tremors*, and Jeff helped mechanize the giant worms and their tentacle tongues. A couple of years later he was back at ADI working on sophisticated Animatronics for the movie *Wolf.* Having gained extensive experience in hydraulic characters at other studios, Jeff returned to ADI for *AVP*, where he built the mechanism for the hydraulic Alien Warrior. As a kid, Jeff was inspired by the film *Planet of the Apes*, and now has his own kids, Jessica and Jason, who, along with his wife Betsy, are his "biggest fans and harshest critics."

01 Even without its gruesome exterior, an Alien facehugger is a rather unnerving sight.

02 Like a modern-day Dr. Frankenstein, Brian Jaecker-Jones is hard at work to bring horror and mayhem to life via an Animatronic facehugger.

03 To rehearse a scene from the script involving an Animatronic facehugger puppet, Joe Pepe (lying on the floor) bravely risks his future ability to have children. Dave Penikas, Seth Hays, Rick Lazzarini, Enrique Bilsland, Lon Muckey, and Johnnie Spence puppeteer the facehugger as Alec Gillis shoots test footage.

04 Spencer Whynaucht creates his own Fourth of July display on a grinding wheel. Kids, note the safety glasses!

05 The removal of an access panel reveals a glimpse into the innerworkings of Predator weaponry.

06 Lon Muckey and Johnnie Spence perform a motion test on a radio-controlled Predator mask to see if it is functioning properly.

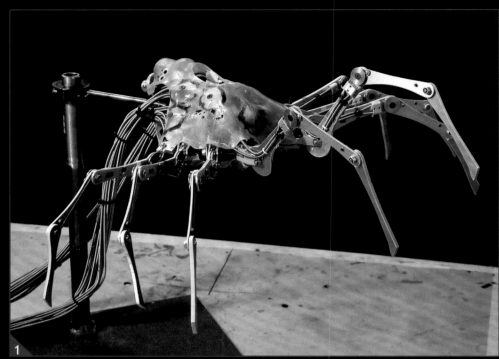

3

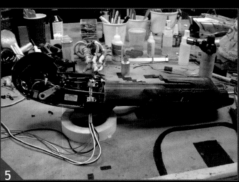

4

5

6

ARTIST PROFILE

BRIAN JAECKER-JONES
Mechanical Designer

In his last year of high school, Brian finally began to think about life after school. *Jurassic Park* caught his attention with the sheer scale and weight of the Animatronic dinosaurs. "They were just so present and real." In college, he studied mechanical design and worked backstage on theater productions, ultimately building his own Animatronic squirrel character as his senior project (now *that's* scary). With a love of combining the illusions of theater with mechanical engineering, Brian landed his first job within a year of graduating college. His key work on the hero Animatronic facehugger earns the utmost of respect at work, but it is his new son, Charlie, with his wife, Amy, that is his greatest work to date.

JOHNNIE SPENCE
Mechanical Designer

Johnnie was born in England and found early inspiration in Rick Baker's *American Werewolf in London* and *Thriller*. Experimenting with make-up on his mom and his sister (and anyone he could get his hands on), he didn't find school to compare as a source of interest. At fifteen he landed his first job as a sculptor and painter but soon gravitated toward mechanical design and fabrication. Fifteen years later, Johnnie is still excited by the challenges of each new project. His first experiences with us on *Bedazzled* and *Scary Movie 3* ended up being cut from the films. But on *AVP*, he articulated the hero Predator Animatronic heads, giving them a range of movement and expression beyond what has been seen previously. Try cutting those out!

01 Initially, a crude Alien Queen was mocked up out of unfinished pieces to get a rough approximation of her size. Andy Schoneberg and Tom Woodruff, Jr. provide arm support and scale reference.

02 Seen from the rear, a row of heavy-duty counterweights extend from the hydraulic queen's wheeled base to provide her with stability and balance.

03 The *Starship Troopers* Brain Bug and Brian Namanny observe as Steve Rosenbluth gives the queen's Animatronics an early test run.

04 Her sheer size provides ample room and opportunities for Mark Irvin, Rob Derry, and George Bernota to get involved.

05 Lead Hydraulics Designer Marc Irvin works on the beast's inner neck mechanisms.

06 NHL goalie or Pittsburgh steel-worker? How about monster-maker extraordinaire? Marc Irvin takes his welding torch to the queen.

07 George Bernota works on the queen. The light-colored fiberglass shell will provide support for the foam latex skin that will eventually be added.

08 George Bernota somehow makes sense out of a plethora of wires and servo valves near the base of the queen.

ARTIST PROFILE

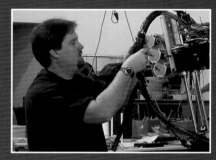

MARC IRVIN
Lead Hydraulics Designer

After attending Cal Poly Pomona, Mark started a car restoration company and things were fine. Then, he took a tour of an Animatronics studio. He was a kid in a candy store; only this candy was steel and stuffed into the skin of some nightmarish creature, like a high voltage piñata. Mark had a newfound need to build creatures of mass destruction. He has also worked at ADI on *Evolution* and *Santa Clause 2.* He's proud of the Queen Alien that performed for two months without any structural failure. Mark's biggest pride: his wife Karen and daughters Kendall and Jenna. His secret desire is to build robots that don't get covered up with a skin, so you can see his mechanisms. Sweet steel candy (coincidentally, that was the name of his rock band in junior high).

GEORGE BERNOTA
Mechanical Designer

With a degree in mechanical engineering from Worcester Polytechnic Institute, George had built a varied resume of professional experiences. The list of films that wowed George and inspired him to work in films is no less varied: *2001: A Space Odyssey, Brazil, Dr. Zhivago,* and *North by Northwest.* Eventually George made his way into the Animatronic field and has worked on such films at ADI as *Mortal Kombat, Jumanji, Alien Resurrection, Starship Troopers, My Favorite Martian,* and *Castaway.* AVP was a real test to be able to create the complex Alien Queen in such a short period of time with such resounding success. He lives in Los Angeles with his wife, Rachel Kelley, and their son, Gus.

6

5

7

8

01 "That'll teach you!" George Bernota wrenches the hydraulic queen into submission.

02 Probably one of the most feared tongues in all of science fiction, the Alien Queen's oral appendage is not one to be messed with.

03 Even without her skin, her "Alien" qualities are beginning to show.

04 Two of the many denizens of the ADI machine shop, Alex Richardson and Enrique Bilsland. Most of the pieces that make up ADI's elaborate Animatronics are custom-made on site.

05 Brian Namanny and a camera-shy Marc Irvin fasten a carapace to the queen for an early test fitting.

ARTIST PROFILE

SETH HAYS
Mechanical Designer

Seth was born in Albuquerque, as the second of five children to parents who were very supportive of his interests in special effects. While attending art school in Colorado, Seth was fascinated by special effects behind-the-scenes stories. He knew that L.A. was the place to be and moved to continue his art education there. The opportunity to intern under Dave Penikas in our mechanical department was a proving ground for his mechanical skills and his abilities to think quickly and efficiently, and he soon amassed a sizeable resume. With the ability to fluctuate between both the mechanical and art departments with success, Seth has proven himself to be a very talented, well-rounded artist and technician, who still manages time for his sculptural art as well.

ROB DERRY
Mechanical Designer

They start 'em young in the Derry family. Rob's dad, Kim, is an effects technician who taught his son to weld at age 10. After a tour of duty in the Air Force, Rob joined his brother, Glenn, and uncle, Jim, in the movie business, after being inspired by Stan Winston's work in *Jurassic Park.* Before *AVP,* Rob worked at ADI on *The Santa Clause 2,* taking the first manned flight of Comet the flying reindeer, which he helped build. Rob calls the Queen Alien "the most complex and powerful machine I have ever had the pleasure of being involved with." During *AVP,* Rob celebrated his first anniversary with his wife, Michelle. We don't know if they are planning children, but Rob often thinks about getting a little Derry heir.

1 A team of seven puppeteers power up the queen in order to shoot a test footage "status report" for Director Paul W. S. Anderson.

The hydraulic Alien Queen's movement controls were divided as follows:

One puppeteer handled the movements of the face and jaw (and striking tongue if necessary).

Another worked the gross movements of the neck and head.

One controlled the torso.

The lips were radio-controlled by another puppeteer.

Each of her large arms required a separate operator.

One person controlled the broad movements of her pair of smaller arms while others controlled the fingers on those arms.

The back spines were operated by yet another puppeteer.

Finally, one person manned the control computer monitoring the electrical and hydraulic systems, activating any pre-recorded movements, and was in charge of the fail-safe safety system.

If required by the scene, additional crew members handled drool, blood, and steam functions as well as moving her along on a dolly track.

2 With mechanic telepathy (and a little practice) Rob Derry, Steve Rosenbluth, Brian Jaecker-Jones, George Bernota, Bob Mano, Marc Irvin, and Lon Muckey work in unison to bring the Alien Queen to life.

3 A frightening scene even in a well-lit shop and without the scream. Note that the condoms used for jaw tendons have only been attached on one side so far.

Opposite: Engrossed in his work, Don Krause tests some wiring that will ultimately help bring ADI's monstrosities to life.

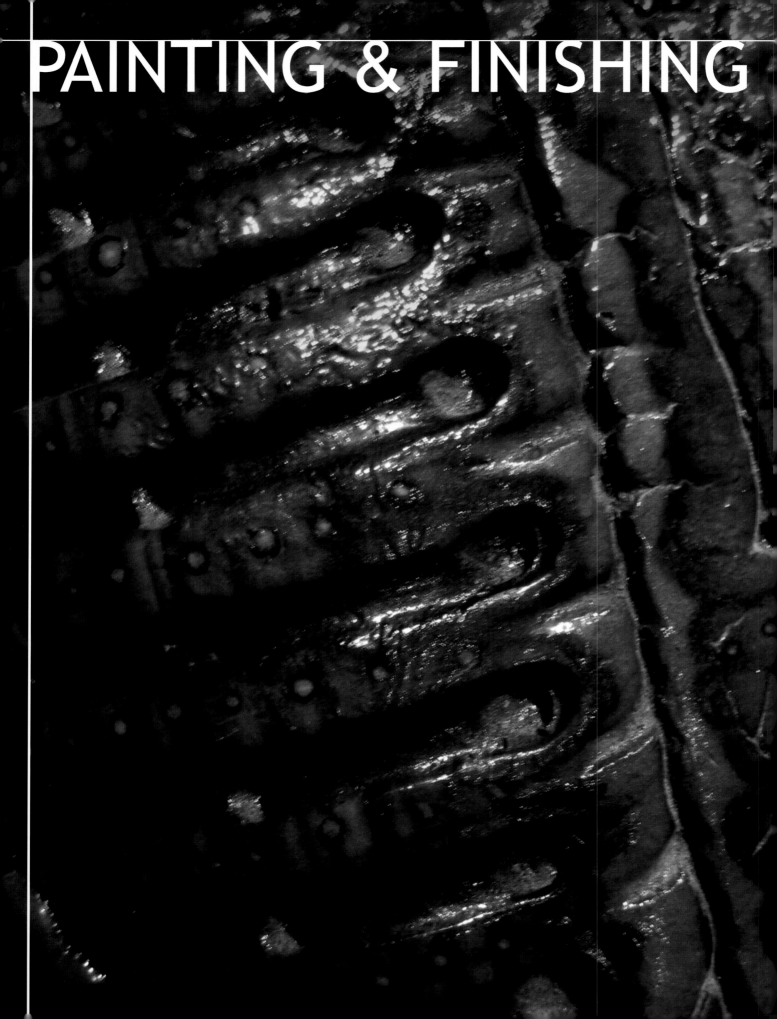

PAINTING & FINISHING

We're Going to Need A Bigger Brush

The paint schemes for all the creatures had been well established with audiences already. For the most part, Alien eggs, face-huggers, chestbursters, and even the queen herself would remain true to what had already been seen in earlier films. For the warriors and the lead Predator, Scar, there would be some subtle variations to accomplish the design goals chosen at the beginning of the process.

The queen was first introduced in *Aliens* with an almost iridescent blue highlight scheme. This design worked well, especially under Cameron's bluish-cast lighting scheme. When she appeared again in *Alien Resurrection*, a blend of pearlescent paints were used, incorporating brown and green tones into her overall appearance. This gave a shimmery bug-like quality to her surface. This time around, we chose to go back toward her original color and once again created a color scheme of rich blacks in the deeps and blues and silvers for highlights.

The Alien Warrior, in the last two films stayed in a palette of warm siennas and brown tones, emulating the feeling of Giger's original artwork as it was published in his book, *Necronomicon*. For *AVP*, Paul Anderson wanted to return to the deeper blacks of the original film. Production Designer Richard Bridgland's pyramid interiors were black, obsidian-like blocks, and the Aliens needed matching tones in order to integrate into their surroundings.

A simple black finish wouldn't pick up the light properly and the Alien would lack any characteristic definition, so a reflective silver highlight scheme was devised to help define the shapes of the Alien. Some gold and subtle blue tones were also introduced to avoid a totally monochromatic look. By the time slime was applied to the suit on set, the distinctive Alien imagery was complete.

The color scheme of the Predators became subtly warmer and less amphibian in the flesh tones, in keeping with our efforts to make Scar less of a monster, and more of a character. All sixteen Predator body suits were painted identically, so that any of them could be used as a replacement or double at any time. We just didn't know how much abuse the suits would take, so individualizing of characters came via the differences in armor mask design, weaponry, and body armor. At the time we wrestled with the decision of body uniformity, wondering if we were cutting too many corners, but as we began shooting it was clear we'd made the right decision. The physical demands on these suits were intense.

As rough as the fight scenes were on the foam latex Predator bodies, the body armor took most of the abuse. Some armor pieces were fiberglass, but most were semi-flexible urethane parts painted with a special plasticized paint system that combined a convincing metallic luster with a tenacious durability. There were over five hundred individual armor pieces created for *AVP*.

Above: A Predator shuriken, lethal *and* beautiful.
Opposite: An extreme close-up of an Alien thigh shows some of the intricate textures and painted details that adorn one of sci-fi's baddest baddies.

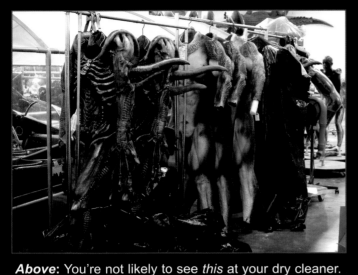

Above: You're not likely to see *this* at your dry cleaner.

Below: Ginger Anglin and Mike Larrabee at work painting the queen. Because its presence would soon be requested in Prague, the final painting, detailing, and mechanical adjustments all happened simultaneously.

The high number of Predator pieces presented an enormous challenge to the fabrication department. They were in charge of taking the foam suits and making them wearable. Nipping, tucking, adding zippers, and reinforcing was work as usual, but the interchangeability factor added greatly to the process. That went for the Alien suits as well. Any given pair of hands, heads, feet, tails, etc., had to match any given Alien body suit. And any given Predator armor piece had to match its corresponding mates as well. Keeping track of all these separate parts was no small challenge.

Because of the demands of the shooting schedule and the high degree of physicality required of the Alien Warrior in *AVP*, we opted to streamline the suiting and unsuiting process. Previously we had actually glued Tom into the suits, which helped maintain a sleek look to the Alien. This time we devised closures that allowed Tom to suit and unsuit quickly, so that he could rest more easily in downtime. Adding zippers to get in and out

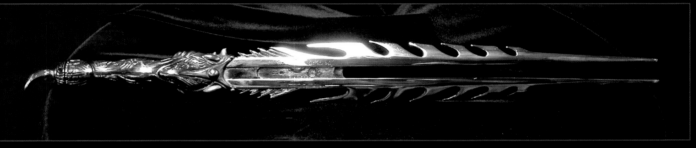

of a rubber suit may sound obvious, but we had always resisted that because of the concern over zipper bumps and unsightly seams. To solve this we created low relief sculptural details that effectively hid the closures. Tom was thrilled at the development, because it meant he could actually eat at lunch, and go to the restroom whenever he pleased. Ah, the simple joys of life.

Top Left: ADI constructed Predator spears both with extended and retracted shafts. Transitions between the two would be handled as a digital effect in post production.

Top Right: Feet. Lots and lots of feet.

Above: Some of the Predator weapons, such as this ceremonial dagger, were chrome-plated for an authentic sheen.

Right: Dawn Dininger applies facial spines to a Predator stunt dummy.

01 Justin Raleigh (in background) and Dave Selvadurai at two different stages in laying down the Alien egg color scheme.

02 A finished Alien egg. Several cable-operated hero eggs, capable of opening and closing their four "lip laps," were used for *AVP* as well as many non-articulated ones.

03 An Alien facehugger.

04 Dave Selvadurai takes proper safety precautions by wearing a respirator mask and painting in a spray booth.

05 A pair of freshly minted facehuggers wait for an unsuspecting lifeform to come just a little closer.

3

4

5

MIKE LARRABEE
Paint Supervisor

If it weren't for Mike's bad driving, he might not be in this book. At age 20 he was hired at ADI as a P.A. (Production Assistant, not Piss Ant...), and promptly crashed his car while on a run. As we were short-handed in the Paint Department, Mike landed a job there mixing paint for "real" painters on *Starship Troopers*. He was a fast learner and soaked up as much info as he could, and lo these nine years later, he's worked on ADI films such as *Alien Resurrection, The X-Files Movie,* and *Evolution.* Mike's earliest inspirations came from the pages of Fangoria magazine, imitating many of the blood and guts effects he saw depicted there. Now that he's the lead painter, he does the airbrushing...and someone else does the driving.

DAVE SELVADURAI
Painter

Dave is a gifted, self-taught artist. Luckily for us, beyond honing his talents, he also taught himself to be flexible, efficient, and a pleasure to work with. A veteran of ten years in the make-up effects industry, he has spent some of that time at ADI on *The X-Files Movie, Spider-Man* 2, and of course *AVP* (Ten years and only three movies with us?! *Who* has he been spending the rest of his time with?). Dave is pursuing his desires to create a comic/children's book ministry, thanking the Lord Jesus Christ for blessing him with talent and inspiration, and his wife, Nichole, for her love and support.

01 In this photo of a painted Alien head, one can see how the heads of the Alien performers actually sit inside the creature's neck. The Alien head, attached securely to the actor's head by a fiberglass skull cap, becomes almost an odd-looking hat.

02 Like a pair of creepy spectators, inanimate Alien stunt dummies sit amidst the commotion of the shop.

03 An Alien chestburster made out of silicone rubber.

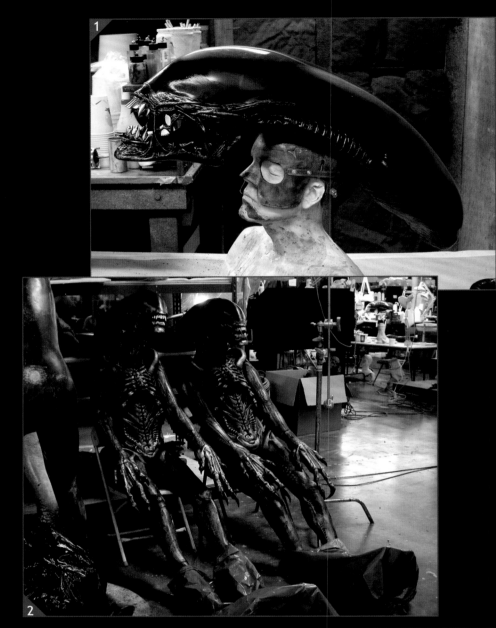

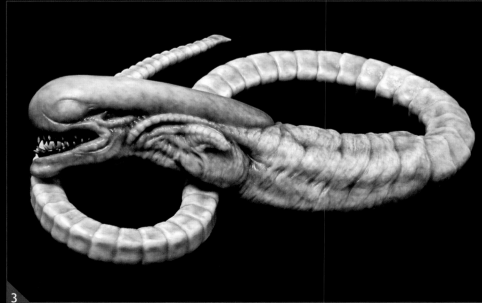

04 The finished Alien Warrior brain prop, fashioned in silicone. Portions of the paint job were done intrinsically, with thin layers of tinted silicone gradually applied to mimic the translucent qualities of natural skin tissue.

05 A close-up view of the brain's posterior lobe.

06 Dave Selvadurai paints a queen torso using a palette of blues, blacks, and silvers.

4

5

6

01 Multiple versions of the queen's head had to be made to accommodate her transition from a pristine condition to a heavily scarred and battle-damaged look. This image shows the underside of a pair of third-scale heads.

02 ADI created Alien Queens in three different sizes for *AVP*. The smallest head is at quarter-scale while the two slightly larger heads are for the third-scale rod puppet. The two largest heads belong to the full-scale hydraulic queen.

03 Ginger Anglin provides a good sense of scale to the queen's sizable armspan.

04 A close-up of the quarter-scale queen rod puppet.

05 The quarter-scale Alien Queen rod puppet.

4

5

JUSTIN RALEIGH
Painter

As a child, Justin was inspired by the make-up of *The Exorcist, The Thing,* and *American Werewolf in London.* He taught himself the craft and at sixteen was a professional make-up artist for print and fashion. By nineteen he was teaching others at the Joe Blasco Make-Up Center, Hollywood, where he earned an honorary diploma. Justin has been a big part of ADI on *Hollow Man, The Sixth Day, Bedazzled,* and *Spider-Man.* On *AVP,* he worked as a sculptor, painter, and researched and developed a new paint system to give plastic and urethane pieces the look of real, aged metal. He was then rewarded by having to *use* that system and oversee the painting of over five hundred pieces of Predator armor in less than a month!

MIKE MANZEL
Painter/Sculptor

With his diverse background it isn't surprising that Mike worked in many different departments at ADI. He's got a degree in advertising, worked in animation, made commercials — and all in Florida. Eventually movies beckoned and he moved to…*Georgia,* where he worked on *Dawson's Creek.* Then movies beckoned louder and he moved all the way to L.A. *Spider-Man* and *Scary Movie III* are a few of Mike's ADI movies. On *AVP* Mike was a mold-maker, a sculptor, and a painter, contributing to the miniature Queen Aliens in all those areas. Mike is married to Karen, from the Finishing Department, where he never works. That's so that when they get home they can still ask each other, "How was your day?"

01 While many Americans travelled down under to work in New Zealand on *The Lord of the Rings*, Brieana Bellis, a native Kiwi herself, returns the favor by lending a helping hand in the ADI Paint Department.

02 Ian Whyte models a pair of scleral contact lenses (which cover the entire eye) based on the coloring seen in the original *Predator*. Before filming began, however, these yellows and purples were replaced by browns and golden ochres to elicit more of a noble and heroic feeling.

03 While the glue dries on the facial spines of one Predator head, more spines are ready for the next.

04 When it comes to casting a Predator, size *does* matter. Leticia Sandoval and TaMara Carlson-Woodard help 7'1" Ian Whyte into the suit for the first time. For this initial costume fitting extensive notes were taken as to what worked, and more importantly, what didn't work, so alterations could be made before the cameras rolled.

4

01 Mike Larrabee paints a Predator body skin. Slight changes were made to the color scheme compared to the Predators of previous films.

02 A finished view of one of the Predator Elder's helmets. Effort was made to make the fiberglass helmets appear battle-worn and made from hammered metal.

03 For *AVP* the Predator's throwing disc was replaced by a shuriken with collapsible blades. As with the Predator spear, versions were made both with the blades extended and collapsed, and the transformation was handled digitally.

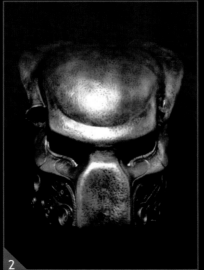

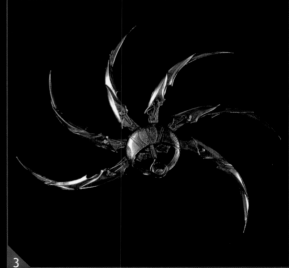

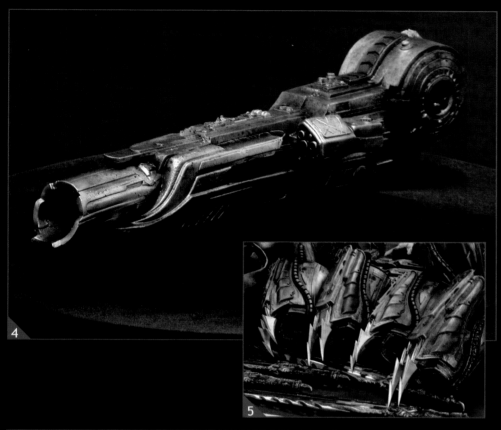

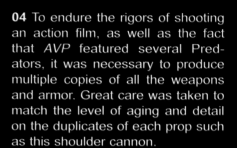

04 To endure the rigors of shooting an action film, as well as the fact that *AVP* featured several Predators, it was necessary to produce multiple copies of all the weapons and armor. Great care was taken to match the level of aging and detail on the duplicates of each prop such as this shoulder cannon.

05 Several Predator wrist blade gauntlets wait patiently for some big scaly hands to give them meaning.

06 Amidst a sea of foam and fiberglass, painted to look like grungy metal, Justin Raleigh inspects pieces of armor before they are shipped to the location shoot in Prague.

To recap, the process of bringing a film character to life is a complex one that involves many steps. Usually a character will be born on a piece of paper on the drawing table (or more and more frequently, its digital counterpart). In this case, concept artist Carlos Huante did a design sketch for a possible new Predator helmet (**01**).

The design process can be lengthy in and of itself, producing numerous sketches that are ferried back and forth between the designers and director (and producers, studio executives, production designer, visual effects supervisor, etc. depending on the particular situation).

Once approved, it goes to a sculptor who develops the design in a three-dimensional form. Bruce Spaulding Fuller first roughs out (**02**) and then gradually adds detail (**03**) to a clay sculpture.

As new design issues arise that were not apparent in a two-dimensional drawing, it is not uncommon for a sculpture to go through many alterations.

1

2

3

After a sculpture has been approved by the director, it is photographed for future reference (**04**) and sent to the Mold Shop to be molded (**05**).

Once a casting has been made from the mold it requires some form of clean-up (trimming seam lines, patching any small air bubbles in the surface, etc.) Steve Munson does this as well as inserting several magnets inside the helmet which will attach it to the foam latex Predator head cowl (**06**).

(If this were an Animatronic creature instead of an inanimate prop, the Mechanical Department would be concurrently designing, building, and testing any Animatronic components needed.)

The next step is a trip to the Paint Department (**07**) before it is finished off with any final fabrication details (such as installing a laser sight and eye lenses).

If all goes properly, the finished prop or character arrives on set, performs well and has a chance to leave an indelible impression on audiences around the world (**08**).

While it is possible for an individual to execute all of the steps alone, feature films with tight deadlines and huge build lists require the collaboration of many talented artists and technicians.

1 Mike Manzel details a Predator shuriken prop to make it look weathered and aged.

2 In a room-sized spray booth, Brieana Bellis paints a Predator's chest armor and backpack unit.

3 Justin Raleigh works on one of many Predator helmets produced for the film.

Opposite: Paint Department Supervisor Mike Larrabee adds the finishing touches to a full-size queen tail.

Hooray For...*Where?*

By the end of October, it was time to leave the frantic pace of our studio and join the production beginning in Prague. Work was still going full steam on the Queen but the shooting schedule called for the Predator and Alien right up front. Two of our eight allotted puppeteers were necessary to the completion of the Queen, so the remaining six of us headed off to the airport late in October.

Weeks of preparation had been put into motion at ADI and a small crew mobilized to get everything we would need for the next four months into crates to be shipped to the Czech Republic. Alien and Predator body suits had to be wrestled from the hands of the painting department to be dressed onto body forms for shipping—we could expect to be greeted by the aroma of paint when we opened the crates at the other end as they were being packed almost as the paint was drying.

A stockpile of materials had been gathered, then picked up, at the studio to be crated and shipped. We had to ship everything we needed, from paints and glues to urethanes, to Alien slime – all to make the journey to the distant location. Shop tools and personal tools also had to be included in shipping records and turned over for proper packaging and shipping as well.

When we got to Prague, earliest indications did not paint a pretty picture. Through a series of mishaps by the shipping company, beautifully finished animatronic Aliens, including our sophisticated

Hero Hydraulic Warrior, sat in crates in Los Angeles under the hot sun of record high temperatures, never making the next step of actually getting on a plane. Other crates slowly made their way as far as Frankfurt where half our crew had to journey by car to help figure out what was missing. Promises of having our things to us in three days were unfulfilled and despite daily updates that things would get there "tomorrow," it took weeks!

We were now down to the day before the Predator was to make his screen debut and we were still waiting for all of his weapons and parts of his costume, which was supposed to be there, you guessed it, "tomorrow." So far, all we had received were some crates of molds and some of our animatronic Alien heads, all transported loosely in a big crate, as well as the Hero Hydraulic Warrior with its translucent dome blistered and bubbled from the L.A. heat. We also had a few of our materials and a bellyful of enthusiasm (or was it the other way around?) so we began to manufacture replacements for the missing Predator pieces. We have a reputation for doing anything – and that's exactly what we did, all through the night.

After a few hours of sleep, we began to dress Ian Whyte as the Predator late the next morning. As Paul Anderson previewed the completed main Predator character, Scar, he was very enthusiastic which was a welcome affirmation of our work and a wonderful pay-off for the long hours the night before.

Opposite: Surrounded by the tools of the filmmaking trade, ADI crew member Tim Leach moistens the queen's slime coating.

Above: Director Paul W. S. Anderson explains a scene to Ian Whyte, playing a Predator Elder, on location in Prague.

Left: Sebastian's (Raoul Bova) day just got worse

After a few scenes of Scar stalking Lex and Weyland up the steps of the temple, it was time for Weyland to unleash his burning oxygen bottle to distract the Predator. We protected the Predator with a coating of slime and fireproof gel then stood back as his shoulders were set on fire in the aftermath. Take after take, the Predator's dreadlocks became increasingly scorched and melted but the overnight work survived.

The frenzied build schedule was now replaced with an equally demanding shooting schedule. Before long, our minimal crew was being split between a main shooting unit and a second unit, shooting concurrently on different sets. Bharat Nalluri directed this second unit, which concentrated on much of our creature work. While Paul was busy concentrating on the main actors and their interaction with Scar and Aliens, Bharat was simultaneously capturing the details of that action, including the key fight sequence between Predators and Aliens in the chambers.

Both units had ambitious needs of Aliens and Predators. Various sets were spread out around town in empty factory spaces which meant fullscale

moves of all Alien and Predator pieces as well as tools and supplies on an almost daily basis.

We were fortunate to have a local crew with some experience to help us throughout the production. In addition, we had been allocated more puppeteers/artists from the U.K. to support us on set and when the production realized the magnitude of its needs, it was responsive to adding to the numbers of people, drawing off additional U.K. talent, most of whom were poised to begin *Harry Potter 3* at any time.

Despite the beauty of the city of Prague, only one set was built outside–the exterior of the whaling town, and even that was because of the scope of the set, not to make use of the beautiful location. Everything else was built and shot indoors. We were on the other side of the world not for its picturesque locale, but because the massive undertaking of the film could be done for a budget.

Throughout the entire schedule there was barely a single day in which an Alien, a Predator, or any one of a huge assortment of creature effects was not shooting on set. To say the least, it kept us busy as we stayed one step ahead of schedule changes and juggled shooting with maintenance and repairs. By the time we got to the major sequences like the first fight between Alien and Predator and the climactic scenes with the Queen Alien, each day had to be approached with precision and the flexibility of knowing things were always changing.

Of course an *Alien* movie doesn't get made without barrels of Alien slime, and to all those crew people on set complaining about the unexpected slime on the floor, on their clothes, and in their hair, we can only say one thing, "Did you even look at the title on the script before you signed on?" Slime is the final dressing and it was everywhere: eggs and facehuggers, chestbursters, Aliens, and of course the queen! Once coated, the monsters are continually freshened up with water, liberally applied from spritz bottles and Hudson sprayers. They may look wet, but they dry out very quickly. This final slime coating serves two purposes. First, it helps highlight the creatures so they can be seen in the dark Alien environment. Second, it also introduces a very tactile quality to the Aliens that is repulsive and works

on both the conscious and subconscious level, taking advantage of the audience's dislike for things that are slimy and generally disgusting.

Being on the set of an Alien picture once again felt like home to us. Whether in London, Prague, or (no place like home) Los Angeles, these movies have been among the defining projects of our career; a career that has spanned twenty years and four Alien features. As long as you, the audience, continue to be thrilled or scared or just find an interest in seeing what happens next, there will be more. And although hard to imagine, it is inevitable that there will come a time when we're not on the set anymore. Many years from now, maybe we'll be sitting in the audience watching someone else's work on an Alien or Predator movie, complaining about how hard it was to find a parking place for the hovercraft. Tom in Pennsylvania. And Alec in Los Angeles.

Above: One badass Alien-killer and one Predator.

Below: Drs. Cheeseman and O'Neil (ADI founders Alec Gillis and Tom Woodruff, Jr. in a cameo appearance) have all the answers. Now if only they could get someone to listen....

01 A once-sacred chamber in the subterranean pyramid has been transformed into a nursery from hell.

02 Something wicked this way comes....Facehuggers emerging from eggs were hand puppets operated by puppeteers reaching through hollow eggs with no bottoms.

03 Paul Spateri and Tom Woodruff, Jr. make sure the Alien eggs are well-slimed.

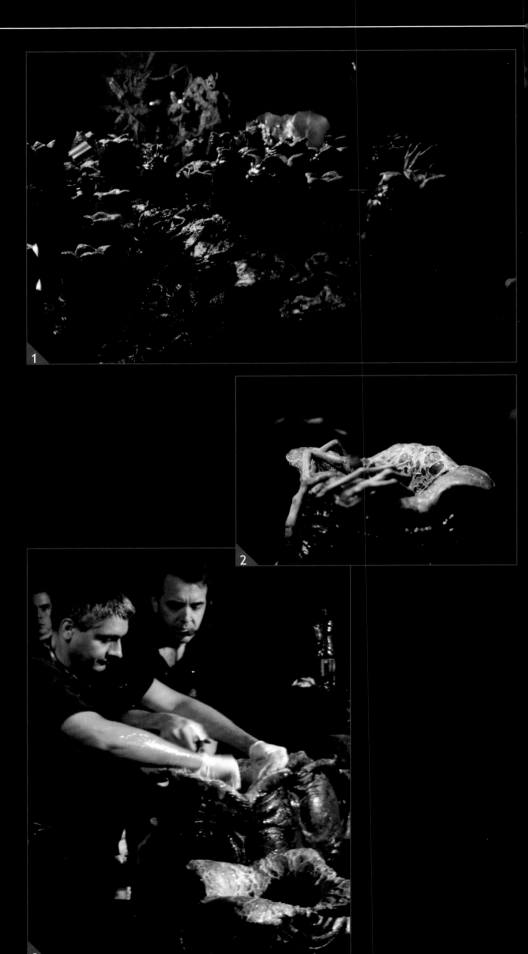

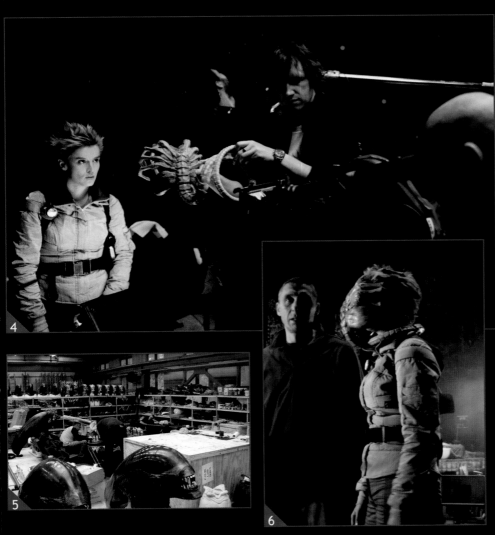

04 "You mean *that* is going on r
face?!" Actor Agathe De La Boula
(Rousseau) warily eyes a facehugg
held by Director Paul W. S. Anderso

05 ADI set up a miniature version
their Chatsworth, California, effe
shop on location in Prague.

06 They're not so bad once you g
used to them...except for that lor
slimy proboscis reaching down t
back of your throat....

07 Under the set Seth Hays inspe
tubing that will soon release amp
amounts of the Predator's signatu
luminescent green blood. The g
was supplied by the Special Effe
Department and is essentially t
same stuff that is in glo-sticks.

01 Which is the better-looking one? Alec Gillis gives his partner in crime, Tom Woodruff, Jr., a spritz to keep his slimy coating moist.

02 The familiar forms of an Alien Warrior are silhouetted by a bank of lights on one of the pyramid sets. In addition to an entourage of men-in-Alien-suits, ADI's Alien contingent also included this hydraulic version.

03 ADI's on set crew prepares for a shot featuring the hydraulic Alien Warrior and a Predator.

04 For a scene where Lex (Sanaa Lathan) fires a piton gun at Scar's assailant, Alien performer Tom Woodruff, Jr. entrusted *AVP*'s Special Effects Department to place directional squib explosives behind his head which were rigged to blow apart the back half of a specially-constructed rigid foam Alien head dome.

Inside The Alien

As a kid, I couldn't tell you the name of a single pro ball player, but I could tell you who was inside the monster suits. I knew which gorillas were Janos Prohaska and which were George Barrows or Charlie Gemora. I knew when the Creature from the Black Lagoon was Ricou Browning or Ben Chapman. I knew which Frankenstein films featured Karloff and which ones used Chaney, Lugosi, or Glenn Strange.

My dad taught me how to throw a football. My mom showed me how to sew fake fur together to make a gorilla costume. I guess that means I was well-rounded. And if any kid ever logged enough hours in front of the TV, studying the monster movies and watching how they moved, it was me. I just never knew it was all going to end up being useful.

When I went from monster fan to monster-maker, I still had the ambition tucked inside to be the monster as well. Despite a few short gigs as radio station mascots and a rental gorilla for publicity functions, I was very shy and a real introvert. It wasn't until I was working for Stan Winston on *Aliens* that the notion of playing a monster in a movie would even strike me.

One night after working late, Richard helped me suit up in one of the Alien suits we built for the film. They were very simple, streamlined builds with raised forms to show bone structures and exoskeleton joints attached to lycra body suits—designed to be seen in the stark lighting in fleeting glimpses. I wanted to get images of a pristine suit before it ended up being worn and ultimately worn-out for the film.

It felt great to be in that suit. I was suddenly aware of the long tail and how much balance it required in order just to be able to hold an appropriate stance. But it worked to my advantage, letting me pitch my weight out in front of my feet and take on a more horizontal form instead of a completely upright man-in-a-suit position. I never did ask to wear the suit in the film, instead thinking it was out of reach and belonged more in the domain of the stuntmen hired for the film. I also didn't think that would all change and I would end up playing the Alien in the subsequent features.

Over the years, I began to add more monster credits to my resume, both in films we did for Stan Winston and later when we formed ADI. With a full set of body molds of myself in storage, it was very practical for an immediate start-up in building a monster suit if I was going to be the one inside.

But beyond the practicality, Alec and I both felt that it would benefit the role. There were often times when Alec and I would work so carefully over the design and building of a creature in our early careers, only to see the final step of a stuntman inside with no real understanding or appreciation of the specifics of the suit, compromise the look onscreen. After all, when we design a creature, we include everything about the character including the way it will move. Having an even higher stake in how successful it all looks on film, I'm also more willing to overlook personal comfort and often used harnesses with no padding for wire work and would spend entire days glued into suits to help preserve the look.

Inside the suit, I can become the monster. It's confining and restricting and many times very frustrating. My attention is always split between what seems natural for the role, and the specifics of what I have to do in a shot, encumbered by a heavy Animatronic head and body suit. Often I see the performance from a perspective outside my mind, watching the creature interact as I try not to look like a man in a rubber suit. I see myself move with the dynamics of a Ray Harryhausen animated creature, both natural and surreal at the same time. And there have been times when the director has said, "A little more Harryhausen in the next take."

It's physically punishing and mentally demanding. There are mornings when I climb into a cold damp suit at six o'clock in the morning. There are the days when I skip lunch breaks because it's less wear-and-tear on me and the suit to get out and back in, in an hour. There are nights when the lights are being shut off and almost everyone has left the stage before I'm out of the suit. Like anything worthwhile, it's hard work, but they say I'm very good at what I do. I hope so, because it's too late to go back to learning that football thing.

—Tom Woodruff, Jr.

01 When Weyland (Lance Henriksen) encounters the Predator Scar on the steps of the ancient pyramid, things go sour very quickly.

02 Weary from their battles down below, Lex and Scar emerge to the icy surface, unaware that their troubles are about to get much worse....

03 Director Paul W. S. Anderson demonstrates to co-Creature Effects Supervisor Alec Gillis his thoughts on how one should wield a Predator's ceremonial dagger.

4

5

6

7

04 Tim Leach threads a straw through a gauntlet of teeth and tusks to give a much-needed drink to a Predator Elder.

05 Doing his best impersonation of a sweaty raccoon, Predator Ian Whyte says, "That's a wrap!" after a long day of shooting.

06 Garth Winkless applies generous amounts of glowing green blood to Scar.

07 United by a common threat, Lex and Scar team up to increase their chances of survival.

117

01 A face only a mother (and hundreds of thousands of fans worldwide) could love.

02 If that's a leash, it must be one pretty big pet. And it is. Scar plays a life-or-death match of tug-of-war with the Alien Queen.

03 Inside the pyramid tomb, Scar is well-attended to by the ADI crew (from left to right: Tom Woodruff, Jr., Garth Winkless, Mark Coulier, Paul Spateri, and Yuri Everson). Although most of the ADI crew was from the United States, a small crew joined them from the United Kingdom, as well as a local Czech crew.

4

04 A Deadly Duo. Predators arri
to stalk Aliens on Earth, but exac
who will be hunting whom remai
to be seen....

05 A Predator quartet (played
slightly smaller-statured actors th
main Predator performer Ian Why
hence their somewhat squ
appearance) works on a gree
screen stage. In post producti
their numbers will be multiplied a
they will be composited into
Predator ship.

5

01 The Alien Queen returns to the silver screen in *AVP*, this time held captive by a yolk and restraints constructed by the Predators (and the Production Art Department).

02 Garth Winkless adds more slime and "yellow matter" to the back of the damaged queen carapace.

03 Tim Leach uses a headlamp to cut through the atmosphere of a heavily fogged set as he adjusts the queen's neck skin.

04 ADI Mechanical Supervisor Dave Penikas makes sure all is well with his "baby."

05 This diva is ready for her close-u

06 The Creature Effects crew dresse
the queen in her damaged state.

07 Remember the mass of wire
and fiberglass shells? You've com
a long way, baby!

01 The Alien Queen makes her point to a Predator.

02 ADI's Animatronic Predator heads provided a wide range of expression and movement.

Opposite: A noble Predator Elder.

Alien and Predator Character Effects
Amalgamated Dynamics, Inc.

Shop Supervisor
Yuri Everson

Assistant Shop Supervisor
Garth Winkless

Mechanical Supervisor
David Penikas

Sculpting Department Supervisor
Andy Schoneberg

Hydraulics Supervisor
Marc Irvin

Paint Supervisor
Mike Larrabee

Finishing Supervisor
Tim Leach

Fabrication Supervisor
TaMara Carlson-Woodard

Foam Supervisor
Roland Blancaflor

Mold Shop Supervisor
Jim Leonard

Foam Supervisor
Roland Blancaflor

Fabrication Supervisor
TaMara Carlson-Woodard

Concept Artists
Chris Ayers
Rhaban Canas
Kevin Chen
Anthony Francisco
Carlos Huante
Joseph C. Pepe
R. K. Post
Farzad Varahramyan

Sculptors
Jeff Buccacio
Akihito Ikeda
Steve Koch
Don Lanning
Michael Manzel
Timothy Martin
David Meng
Michael O'Brien
Bruce Spaulding Fuller

Painters
Brieana Bellis
Justin Raleigh
David D. Selvadurai

Model Makers
Tim Arp
David Chamberlain
Nick Seldon
Erik Stohl

Fabricators
Dawn Dininger
Deborah Galvez
Naomi Gathmann
Christine Papalexis
Leticia Sandoval
Alex Santos

Mold Makers
Mike Arbios
Bryan Blair
David A. Brooke
Toni Buffa
Barry Crane
George Dodge
Johnnie Saiko Espiritu
Davis Fandiño
Peter Farrell
Robert Freitas
Brian Goehring
Christopher Grossnickle
John Halfmann II
Tony McCray

Steven Munson
Gary Pawlowski
David Perteet
Michael A. Rothhaar
Frank Rydberg
Brit Schottelius
A.J. Venuto
Brandon Whynaucht
Neil Winn

Foam Runners
John Calpin
Cory Czekaj
Bill Fesh
Bree Kidd
Matt Mastrella
Brandon Messersmith

Finishing
Ginger Anglin
Brian Clawson
Ivonne Escoto
Jonathan Fedele
Rachael Fionda
Karen Keener-Manzel
Sean Kennedy
Matthew Killen
Junko Komori
Steven Kuzela
Tony Matijevich
Kevin McTurk
Christina Prestia
Nevada Smith
Kathy Sully
Patricia Urias

Mechanical Designers
George Bernota
Enrique Bilsland
Richard Delgado
Rob Derry
Jeff Edwards
Samara Hagopian
Richard Haugen
Seth Hays

Ryan Paul Hurst
Brian Jaecker-Jones
Don Krause
Rick Lazzarini
Patrick Magee
Bob Mano
Lon Muckey
Brian Namanny
Tim Nordella
Mark Penikas
Alex Richardson
Johnnie Spence
Spencer Whynaucht
Chris Wolters
Dustin Van Housen

Office Manager
Tammy Mingus

Production Coordinator
Nicole Michaud

Purchaser
Thasja Hoffmann

Runners
Blake Bolger
Zachery Calig
Colin Gillis
Kristopher Valentine

Special Effects Contact Lenses Provided By
Professional VisionCare
Dr. Richard Silver
Dr. Stacey Sumner
Cristina Patterson – lens artist/coordinator

Predator Helmet Eyeshields Provided By
Oakley
Tim Cadiente – Entertainment Director
Jason Spencer – Special Projects

Czechs Mix
(The Foreign Nationals Crew)

Key Production
Coordinator
Eliska Malíková

Creature Techs
Mark Coulier
Paul Spateri
Stephen Murphy
Duncan Jarmen
Esteban Mendoza
Ivan Poharnok
Richard St. Clair
Simon Webber

Production Assistant
Eliska Petrskovská

Costumers
Vlastamil Práda
Miloslav Císar
Milos Svoboda
Ludek Malí
Jirka Kaderábek
Martin Vitoul

Drivers
Petr Hajek
Petr Havelec
Honza Jary
Milos Kalina
Franta Rousek

Contact Lens Techs
Olina Norková
Stepanká Klimková

Additional Aliens
Rene Halek (stunt)
Radim Vavrecka
Petr Litvik
Martin Stoklasa
Stepán Benca
Tomás Stoklasa

Additional Predators
Heiko Keisow (stunt)
Miroslav Kludsky
Libor Skopek
David Folprecht
Arnost Holovsky
Petr Vorlicek

ADI CONTACT INFO

adiavp@aol.com

To order additional copies of this book and
to view other books we offer, please visit:
www.designstudiopress.com

For volume purchases and resale inquiries
please e-mail:
Info@designstudiopress.com

Or you can write to:

Design Studio Press
8577 Higuera Street
Culver City, CA 90232

tel. 310.836.3116
fax 310.836.1136